THE
RIDGEWAY

Anthony Burton

Aurum

in association with

NATURAL
ENGLAND

First published 2005 by
Aurum Press Ltd, 7 Greenland Street, London NW1 0ND
in association with Natural England.

This revised edition first published 2008
Text copyright © 2005, 2008 by Anthony Burton

The photographs on pages 20, 21, 85, 94 and 104-5 are by Jos Joslin; the
photograph on page 110 is by Greenhalf Photography; and that on page124 is
reproduced by courtesy of the Chilterns Conservation Board. All other
photographs copyright © 2005 by Natural England. Those on the cover and
page 101 are by Martin Trelawney; all others are by Tina Stallard.

Ordnance Survey This product includes mapping data licensed from Ordnance
Survey® with the permission of the Controller of Her Majesty's Stationery
Office. © Crown copyright 2008. All rights reserved. Licence number 43453U.

Ordnance Survey and Travelmaster are registered trademarks and the
Ordnance Survey symbol and Explorer are trademarks of Ordnance Survey, the
national mapping agency of Great Britain.

A catalogue record for this book is available from the British Library.

ISBN 978 1 84513 309 2

1 3 5 4 2
2008 2010 2009

Book design by Robert Updegraff
Printed and bound in Italy by Printer Trento Srl

Cover photograph: *The Chiltern Escarpment from Watlington Hill*
Title-page photograph: *Whitehorse Hill seen from Woolstone*

CONTENTS

Circular walks appear on pages 38, 60, 62, 100, 134

How to use this guide

This guide to the 87-mile (139-kilometre) National Trail along the Ridgeway is in three parts.

• The introduction, with a historical background to the area and practical advice for walkers.

• The Ridgeway walk itself, divided into six chapters, with maps accompanying the description for each section. In general, the sections represent a reasonable day's walk, starting and ending at convenient points, enabling the whole trip to be done in a week, with time to get to and from the area. The distances noted with each chapter represent the total length of that part of the Ridgeway, but do not include any short diversions or circular walks that may be described in that section. The circular walks are all fully described, with their own separate maps. Interesting sites are numbered along the way and points where care has to be taken in choosing the correct route are indicated by capital letters.

• The final section contains practical information, such as how to find out about local transport and where to find accommodation.

The maps have been prepared by the Ordnance Survey for this Trail Guide using 1:25 000 Explorer maps as a base. The line of the Ridgeway is shown in yellow, with the status of each section of the trail – footpath, bridleway, restricted bridleway or byway – shown using the standard Ordnance Survey marking system (see key on inside front cover). This yellow line shows the official line of the trail at the time of writing, but may be different from that shown on older maps. You are recommended to follow this line, which will be the route that is waymarked with the distinctive acorn symbol 🌰 used for all National Trails. Should there be a need to diverge from the route shown in this book, for maintenance work or because the route itself has been changed, then you should follow any official signs that appear along the path. *Black arrows (➡) at the edge of the maps indicate the starting points for those sections.*

Distance Checklist

The following distances along the Ridgeway are included to help you plan your journey.

location	approx. distance from previous location	
	miles	km
Overton Hill	0	0
Barbury Castle (car park)	6.6	10.6
Ogbourne St George	2.7	4.2
Fox Hill	7.7	12.3
Ashbury (B4000)	3.2	5.1
Uffington Castle/Whitehorse Hill	2.1	3.4
Sparsholt Firs	3.0	4.8
Manor Road (for Wantage)	3.8	6.1
Bury Down	5.4	8.6
Compton – bridleway access	2.8	4.8
Streatley (A329)	5.2	8.4
Goring on Thames	0.4	0.6
South Stoke	1.8	2.9
North Stoke	2.3	3.7
Mongewell Park (for Wallingford)	1.3	2.0
Nuffield Common	3.9	6.3
Watlington (Hill Road)	5.6	9.0
Lewknor – road access	2.4	3.8
Chinnor	3.3	5.3
Princes Risborough (Brimmers Road)	4.8	7.7
Wendover	6.5	10.4
Wigginton	6.5	10.4
Tring Station	1.9	3.0
Ivinghoe Beacon	3.4	5.4

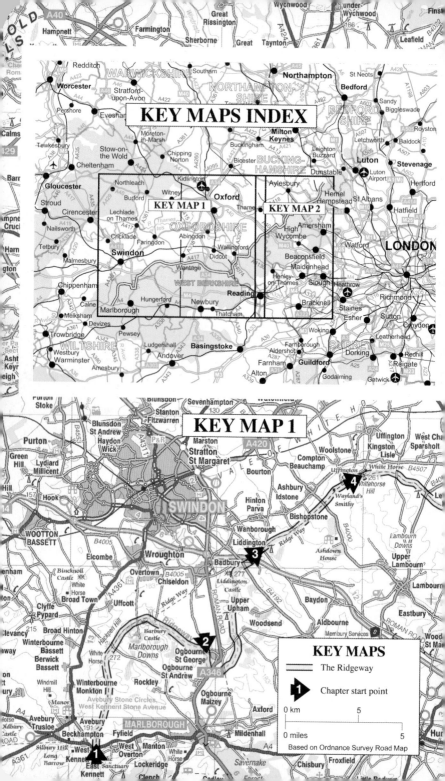

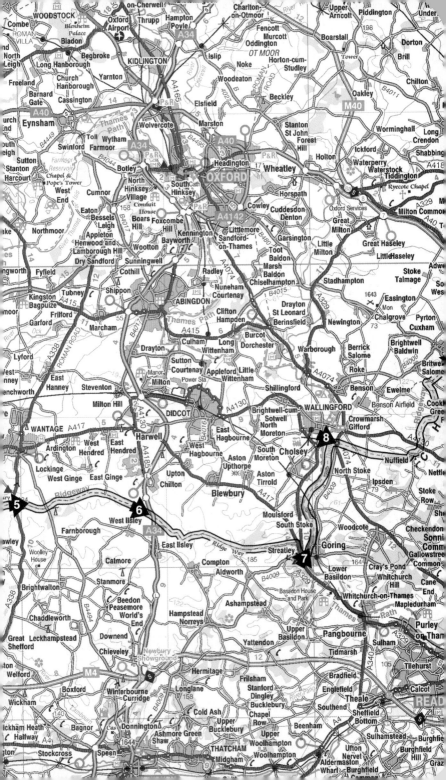

KEY MAP 2

Preface

The 87-mile (139-km) Ridgeway National Trail in central southern England crosses some of Britain's finest chalk downland landscapes. Much of the Ridgeway still follows the same route over the high ground used since prehistoric times by travellers, herdsmen or armies and many remarkable monuments from the past are found close to the trail.

The Ridgeway is easy to follow and can be walked comfortably in a week. Horse-riders and cyclists too can ride the whole of the western half of this trail as far as the River Thames and also some sections further east. For day visitors there are many circular walks and rides utilising sections of the route.

National Trails are managed, promoted and funded by Natural England and local authorities, with the latter also being responsible for their maintenance. The Ridgeway in addition greatly benefits from the work of a group of enthusiastic local volunteers who carry out much of the maintenance.

I hope you will enjoy this book during both your planning and your visit and that it will add to your pleasure in this ancient route.

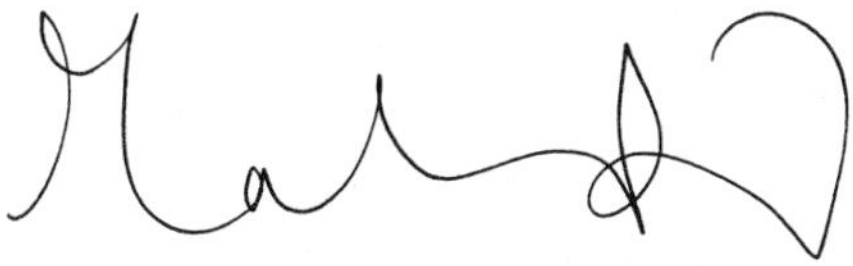

Sir Martin Doughty
Chair
Natural England

Settlements along the Ridgeway are generally found along the spring line at the foot of

...ope, as here at Bishopstone.

PART ONE

INTRODUCTION

The plans for creating the Ridgeway National Trail were first mooted in the 1940s and formally approved in 1972, but that is a mere eye blink in time when looked at in terms of the long history of the route. One cannot even speak very meaningfully of history at all in terms of the Ridgeway, for that implies knowledge that we simply do not have. No one can say just when this became a recognised route, regularly used by travellers. All we can say is that the use goes back long before written records, stretching back not just centuries but millennia (see p.122). Its appeal to early travellers lay in the fact that in general it stays with the high, dry ground of the downs: and that is just as true today. We have no means of knowing whether the earliest people who came this way enjoyed the scenery or not, but the open character of the land and the wide views enjoyed from the escarpment edge are certainly major attractions today.

The Ridgeway offers a journey through magnificent scenery but also a passage through time. The prehistoric monuments are among the finest in Britain, from the country's largest henge and the mysterious barrows of the Bronze Age to the great hill forts of the Iron Age. Very little of the Ridgeway has been surfaced to create modern roads, but it is crossed at numerous places by roads of all kinds, as well as by the great water highway of the Thames, an 18th-century canal, 19th-century railways and a 20th-century motorway. Happily these various transport routes are only occasional visitors and do little to disturb the overall sense of peace and remoteness which is characteristic of most of the route. Part of the western half of the Ridgeway has byway status, which means it can be used by vehicles. In the past this caused damage to the surface, but now the highway authorities have banned recreational vehicles from using most byway sections between October and the end of April and have undertaken extensive repairs. Other regular users of the whole of the Ridgeway are horse-riders and cyclists, though there are sections that are purely footpaths. The western part, however, is open to both types of riders all the way to the Thames. Only walkers enjoy the privilege of being able to complete the entire route, so the following information is largely addressed to them.

Those who intend to walk the whole of the Ridgeway in one trip will need to do a certain amount of planning. The first decision to make is the direction of travel. There is a great deal to be said for starting in the east, so that the end comes as a resounding climax with the prehistoric monuments centred on Avebury. However, the prevailing winds are from the west, and these are the winds that tend to bring the rain. It is infinitely more comfortable to have the wind and rain behind you instead of hitting you straight in the face. I remember all too vividly a day's walking in

One of the immense sarsen stones, dragged down from the Marlborough Downs to create the stone circle and avenue of stones at Avebury.

When the Ridgeway path swoops down the valley it usually arrives at delightful village

re buildings use traditional materials for housing: thatch and timber-framing.

Villages developed at the foot of the escarpment to take advantage of water supplies.

the area of Marlborough Downs when a storm hit from the west and I was walking straight into it, with no shelter of any kind. Even the best waterproofs failed against that onslaught, where the rain found every crevice, blew in under the hood and left me saturated and miserable. I would not recommend the experience. As a result this book is written from the point of view of a walker starting in the west.

The next question to be decided is how long to allow for the walk. Inexperienced walkers might have little idea of how fast they can walk and how far they can expect to cover in a day. A useful starting point is to apply Naismith's Rule, which says that a reasonable average is $2\frac{1}{2}$ miles (4 km) in an hour, but an extra 4 minutes needs to be added for every 100 feet (30 metres) climbed. So, for example, the walk from the start at Overton Hill to Barbury Castle is 5 miles (8 km), so if you were walking on the flat you would expect to be there in 2 hours. But in the course of that walk you will have climbed approximately 330 feet (100 metres), so you need to add in an extra quarter of an hour. It might not seem much, but these times all add up. You only have to decide how many hours a day you feel like walking to get a result for days needed.

Much of the Ridgeway appears as a distinct path, where generations of users have worn away the topsoil to reveal the underlying chalk.

Where once the downland was given over to grazing, today much of it is arable, hence

zzling field spattered with poppies above Bishopstone.

The view from The Ridgeway, looking south over the Vale of White Horse, near Wantage

There is, however, another factor to be brought into consideration: where to stop along the way. Because of the nature of the countryside, the walk tends to stay with the top of the escarpment, while villages snuggle up to the foot of the hill. Those who like to stop somewhere for lunch may find that they have to drop down a considerable way and then climb back up again, adding perhaps an hour's walking time. The same applies for accommodation. You are seldom able to find anywhere absolutely on the route, so do remember that although the distances quoted in the book can be relied on for accuracy, they only refer to time spent on the path itself. So, the next essential is to think about where you are going to stay, and because accommodation can be quite scarce, it is very advisable to book in advance: there is information to help you at the end of the book.

This question of timing is really crucial to the enjoyment of the walk. There is nothing wrong with feeling tired at the end

of the day: there is no fun in feeling exhausted before you get there. It is always advisable to err on the side of caution. Clearly, this is a matter of individual preference. Some walkers pride themselves on covering long distances at speed. Others want to take time out to investigate some interesting site, or simply to pause and take in the views or watch the wildlife. The reader will know which category he or she falls into.

As a general rule, however, one can say that most people will find the Ridgeway just the thing for a week's holiday. You can do the walk at any time of the year, and each season has its own attractions. The disadvantages of winter walking are obvious, not least being the shortness of the days, but the Ridgeway in the snow can be a delight – and you are more likely to have it to yourself! Summer walking creates a different problem, with so much of the Way being open and unshaded, and a hat is sometimes a necessity, not a fashion statement. I have a personal preference for the in-betweens: the freshness of spring or the colours of autumn. There are no hard and fast rules, no 'better' time of year exists, just differences.

Those who intend to be self-sufficient along the Ridgeway will have to decide what they need to take with them. The first priority is to ensure that you keep dry and comfortable, and nothing is more essential than good footwear. Boots are recommended, rather than shoes, as parts of the walk can get very muddy – especially when the land has been used by vehicles after rain. Although there is no very rough ground to cover, chalk becomes very gooey in the wet, managing at the same time to be both slippery and cloying. By contrast, after a long dry spell, the chalk can be rock hard, which can make walking in thin-soled shoes quite uncomfortable. Waterproof clothing is also essential, since much of the walk is over downland where cover is scarce to non existent. Modern breathable fabrics have the extraordinary ability to let perspiration out while not letting water in. Light alloy walking sticks and poles have become increasingly popular in recent years and, though by no means essential, they have two useful functions: they spread the body weight and are valuable as aids for keeping upright on slithery slopes. Like a lot of walkers who had managed without such aids for many years, I was sceptical, but have become a complete convert. Because of the open nature of the walk, many will find it more convenient to take food and drink along rather than make long detours. Everyone has a personal taste in these matters, but the one essential is to have enough liquid – and I have always found a flask of ordinary tap water perfectly acceptable. Some like a mini-feast along the way: others might prefer something as simple as an energy bar to nibble. It is a matter of individual choice. You are not going to die of starvation on the Ridgeway.

The only maps you will need to find the way are the ones in this book, but in order to make the most of them you need a compass. The route is generally clear, but it is by no means unknown for mist to come down or low cloud to cover the tops, and in these circumstances it is very easy to lose all sense of direction. Many walkers find that there is a lot to be said for supplementing the 1:25 000 maps in the book with a set of the Landranger 1:50 000 maps. These are particularly helpful in identifying distant places and landmarks when visibility is good.

Everyone hopes for a trouble-free walk, but things do sometimes go wrong. A simple first aid kit is often useful in patching up cuts and grazes, and it is always worth carrying something with which to treat blisters. A more serious accident may be beyond treating on the spot. For those walking in groups, someone can always be sent to summon help. The mobile phone has proved a great boon, but reception cannot be guaranteed, so everyone should have some back-up system in place. In the first place, make sure that someone knows where you should be at the end of the day, and make arrangements to make contact when you have arrived, so that authorities can be called in if you fail to appear. This is essential for those who walk alone. There is nothing wrong with walking alone: I do it all the time, but it does require extra care. If you really are immobilised, then you want to be found as soon as possible, and one way to make the rescuers' job easier is to have a whistle. This is not a dangerous walk, and there is no reason to suppose things will go wrong, but it is only common sense to be ready in case.

It is not very cheerful to dwell on possible accidents, so to end this introduction let us turn to a far more pleasant topic. What sort of walking experience does the Ridgeway offer? Perhaps one of the best indications of what visitors can look forward to, is the fact that the route lies within two regions officially designated as being Areas of Outstanding Natural Beauty, the North Wessex Downs and the Chilterns. Although essentially the route runs, as the name suggests, along a chalk ridge, that does not mean that there is no variety in the scenery. The beginning, across Marlborough Downs, is exhilarating: a walk in open country of swelling hills and wide vistas. As the route swings away to the east, the pattern changes. Now you will find yourself walking along the escarpment edge, with immense views to the north across the Vale of White Horse, while to the south there is a complex pattern of dips and folds. It remains very open until the path begins to dip down towards the two settlements of Streatley and Goring, staring at each other across the Thames.

Once the Thames valley has been left behind, and the Ridgeway has resumed its eastward line, the scenery begins to change. You are still following the edge of the chalk, but now woodland is the dominant feature in the landscape. The beech woods are particularly fine, especially in autumn. Nearing the end, the route is no longer quite so remote, dropping down to call in on a number of small towns and villages. Finally, you will reach Ivinghoe Beacon and look out over the flat lands of Buckinghamshire and Bedfordshire. You can then congratulate yourself on having completed a magnificent walk, which began in the New Stone Age and ended at the Iron Age – with most other Ages in between.

PART TWO

The Ridgeway

1 Overton Hill to Ogbourne St George

via Barbury Castle
9 miles (14.5 km)

The start of the walk **A** is in something of a no-man's land as far as modern transport is concerned, but makes far more sense if one thinks of the Ridgeway as a prehistoric track. This is an important site, with a group of Bronze Age round barrows and the New Stone Age Sanctuary, of which very little now remains. The start is right beside the busy A4 and, for those approaching from Marlborough, the round barrows at the top of a hill make a convenient landmark. There is parking space in a lay-by on the main road and by the barrows, but it is not very suitable for those setting off for a whole week. Nearby Avebury is served by public transport and has better parking facilities. One solution to this problem is to include the circular walk described on page 38 and use Avebury itself as a starting point. This has the double advantage of accessibility and an opportunity to visit some of the most impressive prehistoric sites in Britain. Nevertheless, the official Ridgeway National Trail does begin here beside the main road, and this is where the description starts.

The trail heads away from the road following a very obvious track. This, like about one fifth of the route, is a byway, which is accessible to vehicles. In the past, this resulted in damage to the surface, particularly during wet weather. However, in Wiltshire the County Council has banned the use of recreational vehicles during the winter on all sections of the Ridgeway in the county, and has put an all-year ban on the section between Barbury Castle and Ogbourne St George. This coupled with on-going improvements to the track has proved an immense benefit to walkers. The round barrows, old burial mounds, are very much a part of this landscape, and can be seen all along this section of the walk, though often disguised under a tall crown of trees. The views are expansive, and landmarks include the Cherhill monument to the west, standing high on a prominent hill. To the right of that is Windmill Hill, site of a Neolithic causewayed camp, which appears to have been a special meeting place for the people who lived here some 4,500 years ago. It has given its name to the earliest New Stone Age culture in Britain. As the track climbs steadily, dark shapes appear on the grassland to the right of the route **1**, which might just about be mistaken for grazing sheep. Enough people had that idea to earn them the

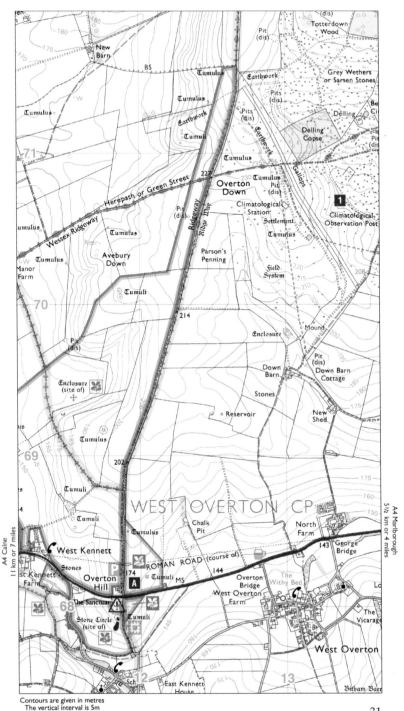

Contours are given in metres
The vertical interval is 5m

31

popular name of the 'Grey Wethers'. They are isolated sandstone boulders, officially known as sarsen stones, and it was stones such as these that were dragged down the hill to create the Avebury monuments. Today, several of these stones can be seen at the side of the track, where they have been moved as part of a process of clearing the land for modern agriculture. Not many years ago this was grazing land, but the advent of modern fertilisers has seen a steady spread of crop growing. There were fields here in prehistoric times, sometimes known as Celtic fields, and slight traces of earthworks, marking boundaries, can still be seen on the modern grassland. They are not, however, very easy to detect by the passing walker, though they become much more evident on a closer look. This whole area of historic importance is now part of the Fyfield Down National Nature Reserve.

Another major track crosses the Ridgeway at this point, known as the Herepath or Green Street. This is a corruption of two names used on Saxon maps – *Here-paeth* and *straet*. The former indicates a military road and the latter seems to refer to a road that has been surfaced in some way. The route remained important right up to the 18th century, when it formed an alternative part of the London–Bath road, between Marlborough and Avebury. The skylark is the bird most associated with this downland landscape. In winter, noisy flocks make forays into the open, but in spring and summer it is the song of individual birds that provides a delightful musical accompaniment to the walk. Round barrows are still very much a feature of the walk, as the track climbs gently and, once past a small conifer copse, a superb panoramic view opens out to the west. A smoothly scooped out valley is just the first of many such very attractive features to be met along the way. Often the grassy banks are marked by lines caused by soil creep, so that the valleys appear exactly as they look on the Ordnance Survey map, with their own built-in contour lines. Eventually the top of the hill is reached, marked by a trig. point on the right. Down in the valley to the north, the view is dominated by Wroughton airfield, now home to the Science Museum's overflow collection, which is occasionally opened to the public. It has an immense range of objects which, when last visited, contained a damaged prototype of the hovercraft. A certain royal dignitary, best known for putting his foot in it, had on this occasion put a foot through it.

The trail arrives at a car park and road crossing, with earthworks which probably represent the remains of a chalk pit. A white horse has been cut from the chalk at this point, but is not visible from the path. The track continues straight on across the road past a stand of beech and another deep-cut valley, this time to the east of the ridge. The Ridgeway skirts the edge of Marlborough Downs, with its rich grassland. Where much of the land has gone under the plough, this has been preserved simply because it supports an important local industry – racehorse training. Gallops have been laid out all over the landscape, some set up with hurdles, others left open. To the north the view is rather less rural, dominated by the towers of Swindon.

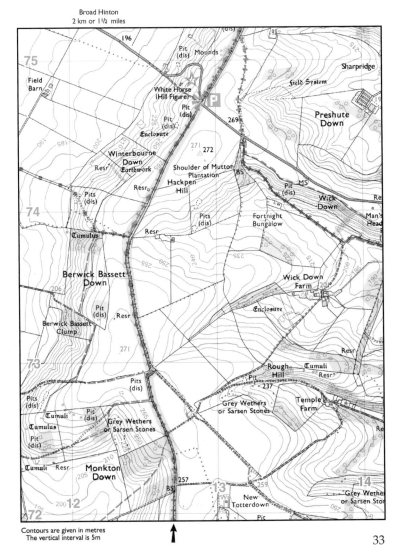

Contours are given in metres
The vertical interval is 5m

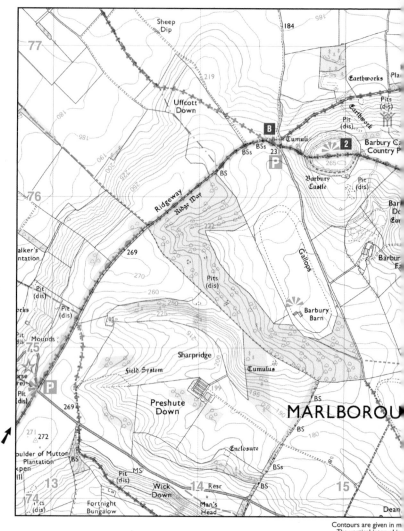

Contours are given in m
The vertical interval is

On reaching the road **B** cross straight over and take the broad track to the right, past the trees, heading straight for the earthworks of the hill fort. The old, original Ridgeway goes left, but the National Trail heads straight off through the ramparts of Barbury Castle **2**. It will be several miles before the two routes are reunited. This immense Iron Age hill fort covers almost 5 hectares, protected by double ramparts, with a deep ditch between. The central section appears to be an unbroken plateau, but aerial photography has revealed traces of huts and excava-

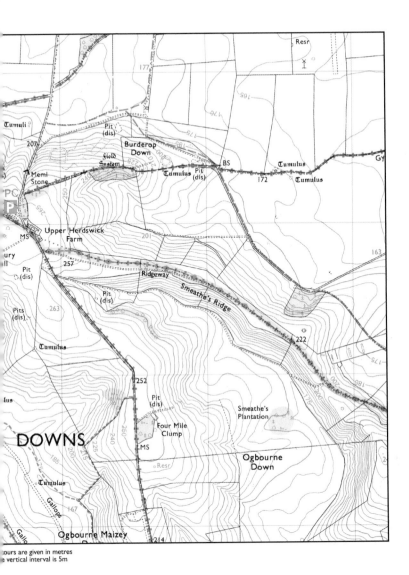

Resr

Tumuli

Pit
(dis)

207

Burderop
Down

Field
System

BS

Tumulus

Gy

Memi
Stone

Tumulus

Pit
(dis)

172

Tumulus

PC

P

Upper Herdswick
Farm

201

163

MS

ury
II

257

Pit
(dis)

Ridgeway

Smeathe's Ridge

Pit
(dis)

263

Pits
(dis)

Tumulus

222

175

252

Pit
(dis)

Smeathe's
Plantation

lus

Four Mile
Clump

DOWNS

MS

Ogbourne
Down

Tumulus

Resr

Gallops

167

Ogbourne Maizey

214

ours are given in metres
e vertical interval is 5m

tions have unearthed jewellery of the period and parts of a chariot. With its panoramic views, the castle was never going to be subjected to a surprise attack. The Iron Age had no written documents, so the name comes from the Saxon chief Bera, a leader of the forces that were steadily pushing the Celts westwards.

Once past the ramparts at the far side, the walk continues on a grassy path, a pleasant reminder of what most of this area would have been like before the advent of modern farming technology. This section ends at a car park, with picnic tables,

Iron Age hill forts are a recurring theme along the Ridgeway. Barbury Castle displays the typical outer defences of ramparts and ditches.

and goes around the back of the toilet block. At the road, turn right, then almost immediately left. Where the rutted track swings round to the right, carry straight on along the ridge at the head of the valley. This is a particularly attractive section, with good walking on a grassy path. The ridge is sinuous, forming a wavering line above the valleys of Ogbourne Down. There are immense views on all sides, and the folded, convoluted hills produce a richly varied landscape. This really is downland walking at its very best, and the walker can continue to enjoy springy grass underfoot where tracks divide swing round to the left, passing a clump of trees on the hillside. At the next track division, continue a short way up the hillside and then turn away from the fence on the middle of three tracks, as indicated by an arrow and the acorn sign for the National Trail. The walk continues past the little Ogbourne reservoir, and then heads downhill to leave the grassland for a broad track heading down to the village. At the road **C** turn right. At this point there is the option of continuing straight on along the footpath which leads to the church on the outskirts of Ogbourne St George.

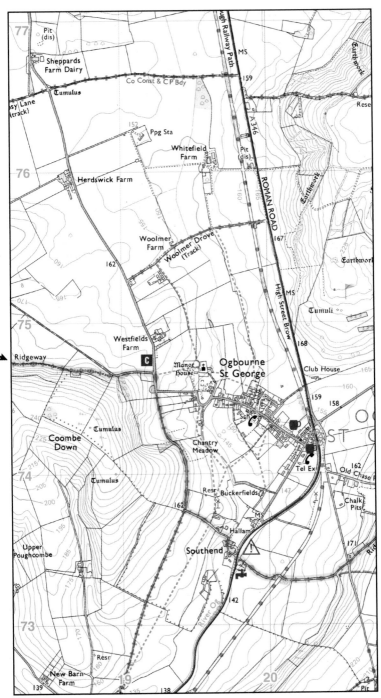

Contours are given in metres
The vertical interval is 5m

A CIRCULAR WALK FROM OVERTON HILL
5 miles (8.5 km)

The walk starts at the beginning of the Ridgeway at Overton Hill, and makes a rewarding alternative first section, as it takes in the three most spectacular archaeological sites of the area. From the start of the Ridgeway at Overton Hill **AA**, cross the main road for the track opposite, signposted as a byway, immediately next to The Sanctuary **3**. This appears to have been a shrine, with a ring of wooden posts, later replaced by stone and now represented in concrete. The track leads downhill towards East Kennett, whose church steeple can be seen poking above the trees. Carry on along the track to cross a stream. The track then leads down to the road; continue on the road to the right through the village.

At the road junction **BB** turn right up the road past the school, with its older school house. The road passes the back of a grand house seen earlier, offering a chance to see the extensive stable block and the high wall, its top protected from the rain by tiles. The church is out of sight down a lane, but the very grand vicarage fronts the road – a remarkable structure for such a small settlement. Once clear of the village, look out for a red brick pump house on the left **CC** and turn left onto a track just before reaching it. Another track comes in from the left: continue straight on for another ten paces, then turn right onto the tree-shaded footpath. At the end of this section, cross the stile and turn left along the line of the fence. Continue straight on across the road and take the path along the bottom of the field. At the next track junction **DD** turn left to West Kennett Long Barrow **4**, which can be seen silhouetted on the skyline. This is one of the biggest New Stone Age burial mounds in Britain, with its chambers roofed over by immense stones.

After visiting the barrow, retrace your steps down the hill and turn left to follow the path up to the road. Cross the road to the wooden gate opposite for a path signposted to Avebury. Immediately to the left is the hugely imposing bulk of Silbury Hill **5**. It is certainly New Stone Age, but no one has yet been able to prove why it was built – and certainly no one has located King Sil, who according to legend sits in the middle in gold armour. Continue on the path by the stream to the road **EE**. Turn right, then cross the road into the car park. Head for the far corner for the path to Avebury Ring **6**. A gate leads into the enclosure, with its surrounding bank and ditch and immense sarsen stones. Avebury henge might not be quite as well known as Stonehenge, but it is considerably larger, encircling much of the old village. Cross the road that runs through the ring and take the path round to the right, following the line of the high bank to reach a gate by the minor road. The henge bank continues on the far side of the road, with an impressive section of deep ditch, but the walk goes right and up the road, which deteriorates into a track. At the end of the barns, at a crossing of paths **FF**, turn right up the byway. The rutted track climbs steadily, and after a while a view opens out to the lines of stones to the west, known as the West Kennett Avenue. The path bends past a clump of trees planted on a round barrow, to make a junction with the Ridgeway **GG**. Either turn back right to the beginning or, if you used this as an alternative start, turn left, having missed only a few hundred metres of rough track.

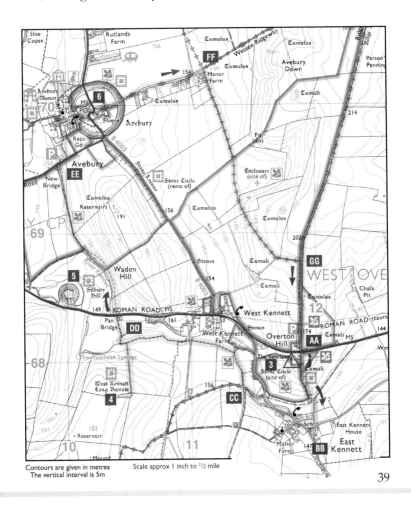

Contours are given in metres   Scale approx 1 inch to ¹/₂ mile
The vertical interval is 5m

The New Stone Age

The Neolithic or New Stone Age lasted in Britain from around 4000 to 2000 BC and plays an important part in the story of the Ridgeway. The Stone Age as a whole lasted for half a million years, from the time when man first began to shape stones to make simple tools such as hand axes. It dates back even before the arrival of *Homo sapiens* in Britain. The New Stone Age was a period when man began to grow crops, keep animals and make hugely impressive monuments. The earliest form of Neolithic culture is known as Windmill Hill, after the causewayed camp just 2 $^1/_2$ miles (4 km) to the west of the trail near Avebury. The site may not look very impressive now, but it is 1,200 feet (360 metres) across and consists of three concentric ditches, crossed by several causeways. The name 'camp' is slightly misleading, since it is unlikely anyone ever lived there, even on a temporary basis, but rather it seems to have been a place for ritual gatherings. Pottery, stone axes and bones – human and animal – were found buried in the ditches.

Stone implements lie at the heart of the culture, and the finest of these were made from flint. You find flint in many places, but the best of it often lies deep below ground. New Stone Age man began mining, not just for the local community but also for trading over a large area. Analysis of the flints from the mines known as Grimes Graves in Norfolk has shown that they were very widely distributed along recognised trade routes. The most important of these routes were the Icknield Way and its continuation, the Ridgeway. Perhaps the men from Norfolk brought their flint axes to Windmill Hill and went back with fine, local pottery. The modern walker can be said to be following in 6,000-year-old footsteps.

The Age is also notable for its great monuments, henges and barrows. Because of the fame of Stonehenge, there is a popular misconception that henges are circles of standing stones: they are not. Basically, they are defined as enclosures, usually circular, formed by a bank and ditch with opposing entrances. The largest henge in Britain, which can be visited on the trail (page 38), is at Avebury. It looks spectacular now, but would have been even grander when first constructed. The bank is over 1,300 feet (400 metres) across, and the internal ditch was originally as much as 29 feet (9 metres) deep. One can only imagine the effect it would have created when the white chalk was visible as a brilliant circle defining the henge. Further elaboration was supplied by sarsen stones brought down from the neighbouring downland and set in circles within the henge. A stone avenue leads down to a mysterious structure known as The Sanctuary. Only the post holes have been discovered, suggesting a wooden building may have stood here.

The long barrows are collective burial places, particularly associated with Windmill Hill culture. The sheer size of long barrows shows the importance attached to the burials, and one of the biggest of them all is very near the start of the trail. West Kennet is a chambered long barrow. The immense mound is over 325 feet (100 metres) long, with an entrance at the eastern end, guarded by two massive stones. Inside is a passageway, with stone chambers to either side. It is all hugely impressive, and a visit to this site is also included in the Avebury circular walk (page 38). Those who do not want to do the circular walk can see the almost equally impressive long barrow known as Wayland's Smithy right beside the main path (page 51).

There is one other important site near Avebury: Silbury Hill, perhaps the most enigmatic ancient monument in Britain. This is a mound built up of chalk to a height of 130 feet (40 metres), and estimates suggest that it would have taken a gang of 500 workers about 10 years to complete it. Its importance is self evident, but why was it built? We simply do not have any idea – or, at least, no idea that can be confirmed. If they do nothing else, the monuments suggest people with powerful beliefs who were very far from the primitive Stone Age men of popular mythology. Those who use the Ridgeway today might like to give the odd moment to think about the men and women who preceded them thousands of years ago.

Wayland's Smithy is a superb example of a New Stone Age long barrow.

41

The standing stones are only a part of the Avebury Sanctuary complex, the biggest he

...nument in Britain – far larger than the better-known Stonehenge.

2 Ogbourne St George to Sparsholt Firs

via Liddington Castle and Uffington Castle
15¹/₂ miles (25 km)

Continue on the road for a short way, until it bends sharply to the left **A,** then continue straight on down the tree-shaded track with the village just visible over to the left. Where the tracks divide **B** turn left towards the road. The path crosses over the little River Og, which seems to be dry even in the wettest weather, to arrive at the hamlet of Southend **7**. This is a most attractive group of buildings, in which tiny windows peer out from under deep fringes of thatch. It is always difficult to date such buildings, as traditional styles lasted through many centuries, but they display characteristics which have been around for many hundreds of years. They are mostly timber-framed, with brick in-fill, but there is also a more local material used for walling: chalk blocks also known as clunch.

Cross straight over the busy main road and continue on the path opposite. The cottage immediately on the right has a drinking-water tap on its wall, kindly provided for use by Ridgeway travellers. The trail passes between the abutments of a now archless bridge **8**, which once carried the lines of the Midland and South Western Junction Railway, connecting Swindon to Marlborough, a reminder of the days when even small villages like the Ogbournes could boast their own stations. Now the old line provides a route for walkers and cyclists, part of an ever-expanding network of old railways that have been put to good use. The track begins to climb as a sunken way, overhung by trees, including some fine old beech. It quite clearly predates the railway age, or there would have been no need to build the bridge. The route crosses over a minor road, which follows the line of an old Roman road, running predictably straight and true. Continue straight on to the track on the far side of the road, which has a firm footing, with flints showing through the chalk. Just what they are doing here is a mystery, but cats' eyes put in the occasional appearance, not at all what one expects on what is little more than a rough country track. The trees end on the left, opening up the view, and the route goes past the skeletal remains of an old wind pump near a reservoir and a former chalk pit.

At the end of a steady climb **C** turn left onto the wide track by another small reservoir, with a rather odd barrel-vaulted, brick roof. The character of the walk changes again, now running on the level through farmland, but still enjoying views over Ogbourne St George and the earlier part of the Ridgeway. On reaching the road **D** turn left by some old coppiced woodland and carry on to the road junction. The route continues on the track opposite. This was once badly rutted, but now shows the benefit of the new regulations and extensive surface repairs. After a few hundred yards walkers can opt to take a narrow footpath through the trees to the left of the track which provides a

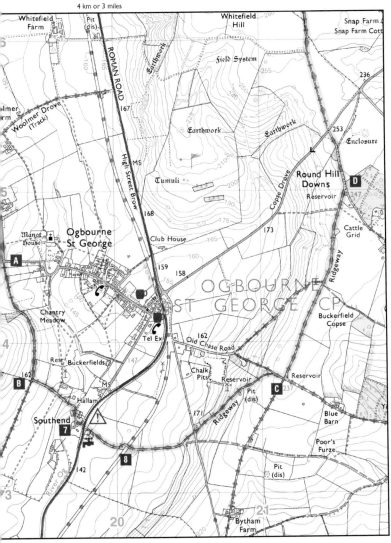

pleasant, if at times meandering, alternative to the main path. This is just the first of a number of such welcome diversions, designed to help the walker. The little path ends, and the route carries straight on along the broader track. At the top of the hill the track goes close by the radio mast which has been a prominent landmark for the last few miles, and which marks the start of a circular walk (page 60). After the next track-crossing, another footpath appears to the left of the broad track, running between hawthorn hedges with a few other trees, including crab apple. Where the trees thin out, there are good views to the west and it makes for a very pleasant section of the walk. The next objective can be seen ahead: the ramparts of another hill fort, with the deep 'V' of the entrance a prominent feature on the horizon. This is Liddington Castle **11** and the route veers towards it.

The rutted track swings away to the right, taking the vehicles off on a detour, and the walker and rider can enjoy the pleasures of a bridleway. Go through the gate at the foot of the hill fort and take the path at the edge of the field. This is very attractive countryside, where, at the time of writing, arable land had given way to grazing – in this case for a large number of horses; the more inquisitive poked their heads over the fence to inspect this break in their routine munching of grass. The route is bordered by a ditch and low bank, which may well have formed an outer limit to the fort. The trail bypasses the fort, which can be reached by a permissive path. A lump in the ground near the earthworks might be mistaken for a long barrow, but is actually of a much later date. This is a pillow mound, an odd name which gives no hint of its function. The rabbit did not appear in England until the 12th century, but the early specimens were not very hardy and apparently were not very good at burrow digging. So landowners who had acquired a taste for rabbit created these mounds for the creatures to give them protection through the winter until they were big enough for the pot.

Liddington Castle stands at the very top of the ridge, with a trig. point to confirm the fact, and now the descent begins. There are good views down into the valley, dominated by the M4 which bends south to take advantage of the gap in the hills. Beyond a gate, the route continues as a stony path heading down towards the motorway. The Celts were not the only ones to recognise a good defensive position when they saw one: a 20th-century pill box can be seen in the middle of a clump of trees on the left. At the road **E** turn left, then right at the next junction, signposted to Bishopstone, and the route of the

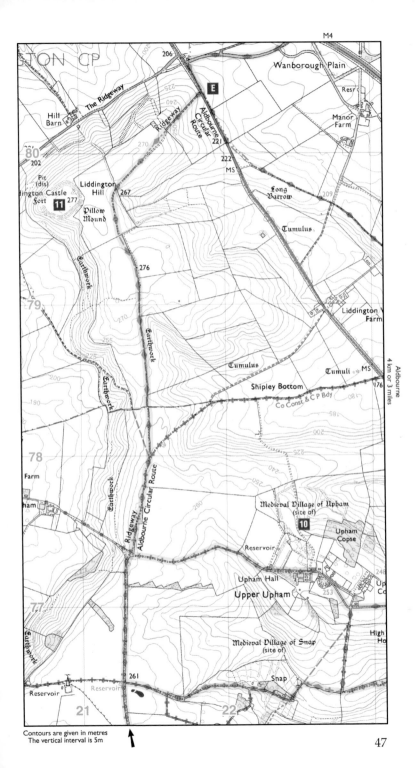

M4

Wanborough Plain

206

E

Resr

Manor
Farm

The Ridgeway

Hill
Barn

Ridgeway

Aldbourne
Circular
Route

221

222

MS

80
202

Pit
(dis)

ington Castle
Fort

11 277

Liddington
Hill

267

Long
Barrow

209

Pillow
Mound

Tumulus

Earthwork

276

79

Earthwork

270

255

Earthwork

Liddington
Farm

Earthwork

Tumulus

Tumuli MS

Aldbourne
4 km or 3 miles

200

190

Shipley Bottom

176

Co Const & C P Bdy

180

185

78

Farm

Earthwork

200

225

Ridgeway

Aldbourne Circular Route

240

250

260

Medieval Village of Upham
(site of)

10

Upham
Copse

Reservoir

248

Upham Hall

U
C

Upper Upham

253

77

Earthwork

Medieval Village of Snap
(site of)

High
Ho

Earthwork

261

Snap

Reservoir

Reservoir

21

22

Contours are given in metres
The vertical interval is 5m

47

Ridgeway is now reunited with the line of the ancient track. Having come down off the ridge, the next climb can be seen up ahead: the shapely cone of Fox Hill. The road crosses the motorway to pass the grounds of King Edward Place, currently home to a commercial advice and training centre. It has all the attributes of a stately home, with a long avenue leading through parkland from an entrance flanked by gatehouses. The difference is that these are modern, and where their 18th- or 19th-century predecessors would have been very modest, they are good- sized houses. At the crossroads there is a pub, The Shepherds Rest, with an unpunctuated name to annoy grammarians. This is the only pub right next to the Ridgeway on the whole of the western half of the trail. Carry on straight across, and after a short way **F** turn right by a stand of mature beech to take the obvious track up the hill.

The next section provides very few route-finding problems, as it follows a more or less straight line along the ridge. Patterns in the landscape begin to appear. Villages are set at regular intervals at the foot of the slope, along what is known as the spring line, where water is available. The lower slopes show evidence of an agricultural system going back for many centuries. There are the small fields, surrounded by low banks, of the oldest communities and the strip lynchets, cultivation

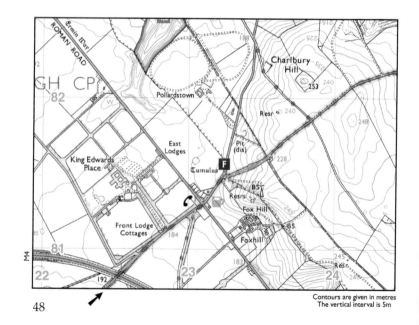

Contours are given in metres
The vertical interval is 5m

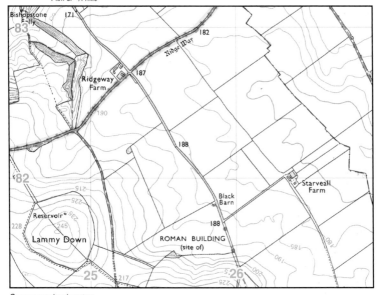

Contours are given in metres
The vertical interval is 5m

terraces on the steep hillside, which are mainly medieval. They are not easy to see from the track, but knowing that the villages are part of a very ancient system helps to put the landscape into perspective. By way of contrast, the dry downland to the south, which was traditionally grazing land, has only a sparse scattering of farms. The open country makes for a good hunting ground for birds of prey, and there is every chance of seeing kestrels and buzzards somewhere along the way.

From the top of Fox Hill, there is a view out over the plain, still dominated in the west by Swindon. The trail stays close to the edge of the escarpment, mostly clearly defined by banks to the side and a straggle of stubby trees and bushes. The views are wide, and a series of paths lead down to the different villages, for those who want to stop for refreshment or find a bed for the night. The one disadvantage is that, having strolled down, you then have to pant back up again. One of these footpaths, to Bishopstone, runs down by an unusually deep cleft, adding a touch of drama to the scene. Cross straight over the road at Ridgeway Farm, and there is an option of continuing on the now familiar wide track or taking the grassy path to the side. Over to the right a colony of pigs rootle among their corrugated iron shelters, though they move house from time to time and may well turn up in another location. Now the track is completely closed in between hedgerows, as the Ridgeway leaves Wiltshire for Oxfordshire. For a considerable distance, as far as Uffington Castle **15**, much of the track continues to have a hard stone surface, as it has since Fox Hill, although there is often a soft grass verge to walk on. In hot weather walkers may be glad to know that there is a drinking-water tap a short distance down the path to Idstone.

Once clear of the hedgerows, the view opens out to the south to a different kind of landscape. Farming mixes with the world of racehorses on the downs above Lambourn, and protection is provided from the elements by long straight rows of trees, planted as windbreaks. To the north, on a good day, you can see right across the Vale of White Horse to the gently rising hills of the Cotswolds. At the next crossing, a footpath leads down to Ashbury, and this is also the start for a circular walk (page 62). The trail continues to the car park at Ashbury Folly, though sadly no folly remains, and carries straight on at the far side of the road. After the next crossing, a short path leads

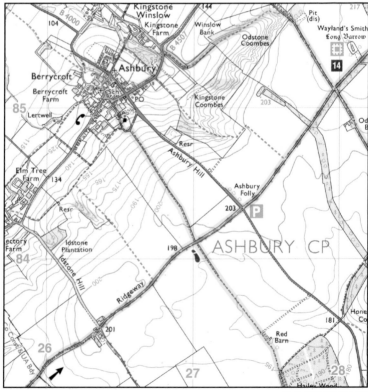

Contours are given in metres
The vertical interval is 5m

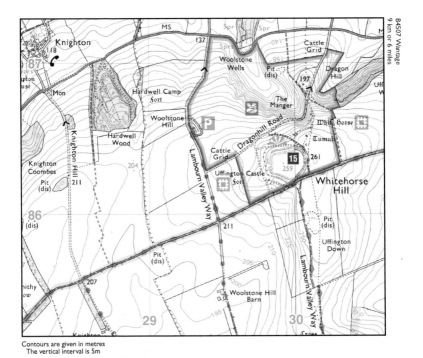

Contours are given in metres
The vertical interval is 5m

down to Wayland's Smithy **14.** This is an extraordinary site, a Neolithic chambered long barrow of immense proportions, created in two stages nearly 5,000 years ago. It was begun around 2800 BC as a mound over 52 feet (16 metres) long, covering a mortuary chamber with wooden walls and a stone floor, which contained 14 bodies. This was then enclosed by boulders and chalk. Then around 50 years later, the much larger mound was built on top of it, with a sarsen kerb all round the outside and flanking ditches. Immense sarsens stand at the entrance, and four of the original stones have survived in situ. A passage then leads to a cruciform burial chamber, where bodies were placed, but for some inexplicable reason no thigh bones were ever found. The name is a corruption of the name of the god Volund, who in legend made the shoes for the Uffington White Horse. Any rider passing this way, whose horse is unlucky enough to shed a shoe, has only to leave the animal tethered overnight, place a coin on a stone and in the morning the horse will be reshod. The result is not guaranteed.

This site acts as an introduction to a section of the trail rich in archaeological remains. Back at the main track, the ramparts of Uffington Castle hill fort **15** appear up ahead. The track

Among the glories of the Ridgeway are the side valleys, their lush hollows bounded by sim

...ssy banks.

The White Horse, created by cutting through the hillside grass to the chalk, has now been shown to date back to the Bronze Age.

climbs up towards it and touches the outer ramparts of this Iron Age fort, which, on the evidence of a coin found on site, was used by the Dobunni tribe. This is an area that almost demands time taken out for exploration, and there is access to the site via a gate. The fort is roughly oval and covers 3.2 hectares, protected by a very imposing set of double ramparts and ditch, the inner bank faced with stone. A little way down the slope, the turf has been cut away down to the chalk to create the highly stylised form of the horse that gives the Vale of White Horse its name. Over the years there have been numerous theories as to when it was originally created, ranging from its being the work of the Iron Age occupants of the fort, to its being cut to celebrate Alfred's victory over the Danes in AD 871. However, in 1995 a new technology, optical luminescence dating (OSL), was used at the site. The outline of the horse was created by digging trenches and filling them with chalk, and OSL showed that the underlying soil had been covered possibly as long ago as 1400 BC and certainly not later than 600 BC. This put the horse back in time to the Bronze Age. It is difficult to make out the form of the horse close up, as it is very large –

over 330 feet (100 metres) from nose to tail – and is best appreciated from the valley floor. After exploring this site, return to the main track.

This part of the trail is set too far back from the edge to get much of a view to the north at first, but the scenery to the south remains pleasantly varied, broken by clumps of trees. The situation soon changes, however, and then there are equally fine vistas over the Vale of White Horse. Beyond another long windbreak of trees, the map shows scant remains of another hill fort, but it has to be said that there is very little to be seen from the path. The route dips gently to the road, which leads down intriguingly named Blowingstone Hill to Kingston Lisle. One possible explanation can be found in a cottage garden at the bottom of the hill. There is a large sarsen stone with a hole, and anyone who blows through it, if they can puff hard enough, creates a horn-like blast. Cross straight

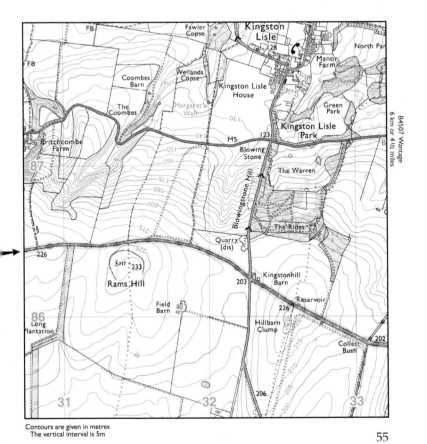

Contours are given in metres
The vertical interval is 5m

over and continue on the track, which climbs again between hedgerows. Where these end, a very attractive landscape is revealed with the gently undulating hills, patched with trees spreading out in all directions. The route now runs above the Lambourn Downs, an area famous for its racing stables, so it comes as no surprise to find gallops, many with brushwood hurdles, appearing close to the Ridgeway. These will remain a feature of the walk for the next few miles.

At the start of the climb up the next hill, there is a considerable footpath detour, which, apart from offering relief from the mud of wet weather, makes a pleasant change from the broad track. The rather steep climb arrives at the top of Sparsholt

The Ridgeway is more than just a footpath; large parts have a higher status, enabling horse-riders and others to enjoy the scenery at Wixen Bushes.

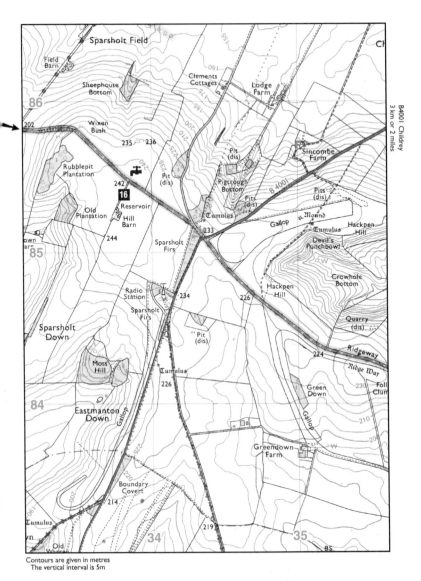

Contours are given in metres
The vertical interval is 5m

Down, which walkers will be pleased to know marks the highest point on this section of the Ridgeway, and the next few miles are marked by no more than a gentle rise and fall. Just before the trees, there is a memorial to a 14-year-old boy, Peter Wren, which consists of an engraved stone and next to that is a very practical tribute to his love of the countryside, in the form of a drinking-water tap for walkers and a trough for animals **16**. This section ends at the road by Sparsholt Firs.

Lambourn Downs was once sheep-rearing country, but now resounds to the thundering ho

...ehorses on the gallops.

A Circular Walk via Upper Upham
6 miles (9.5 km)

This walk provides an introduction to one of the lush valleys, leading down from the ridge, and also takes in a grand house and the all but vanished remains of the village that once stood beside it. Begin at the point where a byway crosses the Ridgeway **AA**, with a communication mast in sight on the left. Turn right down the byway. Where the way divides **BB,** continue straight through the gate to join the broad, grassy track leading towards the wood. Take the path to the right of the trees; there is no shortage of company, as you are greeted by a large, noisy population of pheasant and partridge. The track now heads more steeply downhill, enclosed in the gently folded hills. Immediately beside the track, the wood itself is an attractive mixture of broadleaved trees, and contains a mysterious stone in memory of the children of Snap. Snap itself has virtually disappeared, but originally stood just beyond the woodland. The landscape is pleasantly varied, an undulating mixture of arable and pasture, grazed by cows and sheep. Where tracks cross, continue straight along the path beside the field, which soon begins to snake round another patch of woodland, dominated by some imposing beech. Beyond that is the smoothly rounded hill of High Clear Down, now a nature reserve. The path passes what must once have been a very grand barn, but now looks rather sorry for itself, patched in corrugated iron. Another fine wood runs along the crest of the hill to the right, after which the valley begins to level out.

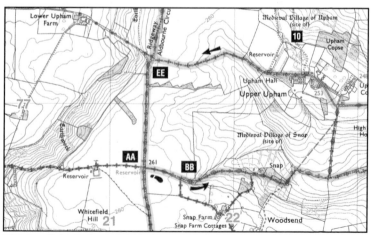

Scale is approx 1 inch to 1/2 mile

Contours are given in metres
The vertical interval is 5m

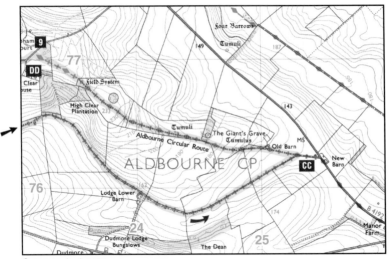

Contours are given in metres
The vertical interval is 5m

At the track junction **CC** turn sharp left on the byway to Upper Upham on a wide track that begins to climb past a line of beech trees. Although the other track is very close, this part of the walk has a quite different atmosphere, with airy views out over chalky fields that seem to be dusted with snow. Just inside the first clump of woodland is a large burial mound, topped with trees, and known, almost inevitably, as the Giant's Grave. Now the path enters an area of very open downland, and over to the right there is a splendid view of a round barrow set in the valley floor. There is now a good, steady climb with very wide views. The path continues past a neat, circular copse and after passing the edge of the next wood continues as a grassy footpath, heading for the obvious break in the trees up ahead. This section ends with a very broad grass track running between paddocks and woodland. At the end of the track Upham Court **9** comes into view – a splendid stone house, with mullioned windows, the grandest of which rise the full height of the façade.

At the road **DD** turn left. Upper Upham seems oddly suburban, with modern houses; the original village of Upham disappeared, probably in the 15th century. All that remain are a number of bumps and hollows in the fields to the right, just past the new development **10**. The road continues as a track, dipping briefly before climbing back up to rejoin the Ridgeway **EE**. Turn left on the Ridgeway, which here runs between hedges, to return to the start; or turn right to continue the main walk.

A Circular Walk via Ashbury
6¹/₂ miles (10.5 km)

Where a footpath crosses the Ridgeway **AA** turn right, and take the path to the right of the hedge. This is a very open landscape, largely of arable farmland, and the path continues down to the woodland. Cross the stile to the right of the gate at the start of the wood. Keep close to the fence for very pleasant walking on grassland, still used for grazing. From the next stile, carry straight on across the field, heading for the earthworks of Alfred's Castle **12**. Cross the stile in the fence to visit the site, which consists of an earth bank and the vestiges of a ditch. It is probably Iron Age, but earned its name from a legend that this was the site where Alfred's forces gathered to fight the Danes in AD 871.

Leave the site by a second stile to continue on the track, and now Ashdown House **13** comes into view. It is an extraordinary, tall, symmetrical block, topped by a cupola. Built in the 17th century, it is quite unlike other grand houses of the period. The walk passes the end of a formal, but newly planted avenue of trees, separated from the fields by a ha-ha. Follow the track as it swings round to the left, passing the farm and former stables, topped by a weather vane in the form of a coach and horses. Cross straight over the main road **BB** and take the path on the left, heading on a diagonal up Weathercock Hill, which takes its name from the weather vane on a high pole at the summit. The path heads well to the left of the landmark, and soon a stile will come into view. The hill offers a splendid view of Ashdown House. Once over the stile, continue in the same direction, following the rather faint green path, indicated by a yellow arrow. Head initially to the right of an isolated group of trees on the horizon; from the top of the hill a marker post will be seen up ahead. Continue, crossing a broad track and another footpath, heading for a signpost on the ridge. At the bridleway **CC** turn left. Keep straight on along this path, heading for the break in the line of trees up ahead. Continue to the next row of trees, which marks the line of the Ridgeway. Here **DD** you can turn left to return to the start; for the longer walk, carry straight on.

The broad path leads on towards a small copse. Just before reaching it **EE**, turn left on to the sunken track, leading steeply downhill to a beautiful little steep-sided valley. Now follow the bottom edge of the line of the trees on the right-hand side. Cross a stile and at the end of the next field turn right and take the track down to the road **FF**. Turn left towards the attractive village of Ashbury. At the hotel **GG** turn left up Church Lane. The church itself, built between the 12th and 15th centuries, is well worth visiting. Continue past the church and, where the tarmac ends, turn left on to the path then immediately right on to the path heading up the hill, back to the Ridgeway.

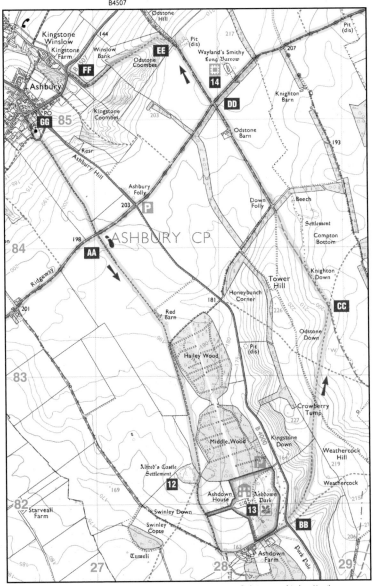

Contours are given in metres
The vertical interval is 5m

Scale is approx 1 inch to 1/2 mile

Geology and scenery

Look at a geological map of Britain, and you will see a great, uniform band of chalk running from the south coast all the way to Norfolk and the North Sea. Set down the line of the Ridgeway on the map and it can be seen to run just inside this band, close to the northern edge. To the north of that again is an area where greensand gives way to clay. It is this juxtaposition that has created the special scenery of the walk.

The chalk was formed tens of millions of years ago, when the whole area was covered by a shallow sea, rich in tiny shellfish. When these died, their bodies sank to the sea bed, where their shells coalesced in the mud, and the chalk was formed. Over the long ages of geological time, the earth has been a place of violent upheavals. One of these vast movements crumpled the surface to throw up the Alps and pushed up the chalk, which rose as a giant dome. It stretched from northern Europe as a continuous land mass, before the sea finally broke through to create the English Channel. The elements have worked at the chalk, crumpling it up and smoothing it out. The result has been the typical landscape of gently rounded hills, falling away at the edge in a steep scarp. The character of chalk has been all important. It is permeable to water, so that rain seeps through until it meets the underlying clay, when it is forced out to the surface. These spring lines at the foot of the scarp have formed obvious sites for settlements.

At the top of the chalk downland, the soil is generally thin, though in a few places it can be overlaid with a thick clay, as

The 'Grey Wethers' boulders on Marlborough Downs are thought to resemble sheep.

walkers unlucky enough to reach such areas in wet weather will soon discover. The soil produces fine grassland, but poor crops, unless aided by modern chemical fertilisers. The result has been that, historically, the downs have provided pasture, mainly for sheep. Watering the flocks has been problematical because of the porous nature of the chalk, so generations of farmers have dug hollows and added a watertight lining. Because they collect dew as well as rain, they are known as dew ponds. The thin soil of the uplands suited the earliest settlers, whose primitive ploughs could not turn the heavier clays of the valleys. But in time, the valleys were cleared of trees and the land ploughed, establishing a pattern still recognisable today, with fields and farms in the valleys contrasting with the open grassland of the downs. The clearing of the woodland and particularly the felling of the oak forests provided an opportunity for another tree to thrive, the beech. The beech woods are a splendid feature of the Chilterns at the eastern end of the Ridgeway.

Another aspect of the chalk's ability to soak up water rather than be broken by it, is the almost complete absence of river valleys crossing the downs. The one exception is the so-called Goring Gap, where the Thames has forced a way through the hills. The chalk, however, is not consistent. Some chalks have proved harder than others, so that erosion has not been uniform and there are folds creating minor scarps behind the line of the main escarpment, dropping away to the plain. The chalk also contains other materials. Flint is common and on the Marlborough Downs sandstone boulders are to be seen scattered over the landscape. They are known as sarsen stones, or in popular local usage as 'Grey Wethers', since from a distance they are supposed to look like sheep. There is ample opportunity to decide for oneself just how sheep-like the stones are.

Throughout virtually the whole length of the Ridgeway, chalk is the dominant factor. Its nature has given the landscape its distinctive shape. In many places the chalk breaks through where the grass has been worn away in tracks and paths that gleam brightly in the sun, but it turns to a less attractive grey goo in wet weather. And this quality of the chalk has been exploited to create chalk figures on the hillside, of which by far the most exciting is the White Horse, which has given its name to an entire district, the Vale of White Horse. Most importantly, it is the nature of the chalk to stay literally high and dry which has made it an obvious route for travellers, from the traders and drovers of the past to the walkers of the present.

3 Sparsholt Firs to Streatley

via Bury Down
17¹⁄₂ miles (28 km)

Turn right up the minor road, passing a copse boasting a number of fine beech trees, and at the T-junction **A** cross straight over the main road for the track opposite. There is a sign warning of low-flying model aircraft, but this is a very minor hazard. The broad green way now runs alongside some of the most imposing scenery encountered so far. The land drops away steeply to the north to Crowhole Bottom and Devil's Punchbowl **17**. It is a curious fact that only the most attractive spots seem to be named after the Devil: England boasts four punchbowls and around 100 other geographical features, ranging from his frying pan to his staircase. This is among the best. The mythology may be doubtful, but the modern age has identified three Sites of Special Scientific Interest here. The track is wide and grassy, following the edge of the deep valley, and swoops off down before rising again to the tree-lined horizon.

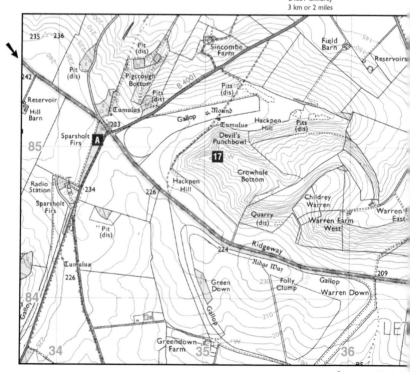

Contours are given in me
The vertical interval is 5

This is rough grazing land, still used for sheep farming, and chalk tracks cut white wandering lines across the hillside. It is well worth pausing to gaze back from the top of the hill to enjoy a last look at this wonderful view.

Carry straight on over the road and another alternative path appears, this time running through a line of trees for quite some way. It is, in fact, a very pleasant walk and offers the advantage of giving a better view than the main track. After the detour, the view to the north is closed off by a dense hedgerow, while that to the south opens out. A path on the left leads down to Letcombe Bassett, but those who do choose to call in at the village will face a very steep climb back up to the main walk. Where barns appear straight ahead, look over to the left and you will see the easily recognised ramparts of the next in the line of Ridgeway hill forts, Segsbury or Letcombe Castle **18**. This is a very large fort, with the southern ramparts running parallel to the Ridgeway for some $^1/_4$ mile (400 metres), clear evidence that the ancient track was already an established feature when the fort was built.

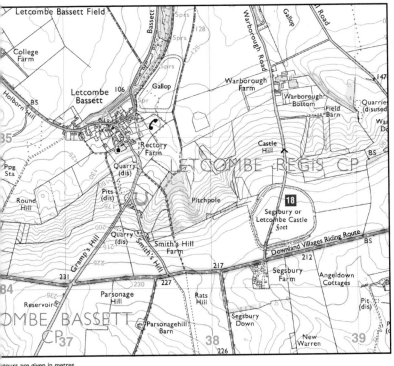

A feature of the Ridgeway is the immense view across the Oxfordshire countryside.

Once the fort has been left behind, another gentle climb brings the track to a house surrounded by a rather surprisingly suburban hedge and the main road down to Wantage **B**. Turn right at the road and then left on the track signposted to White House Farm. There are a number of houses along the way, including an attractive barn conversion. Once clear of the houses, the way enters farmland which in winter looks as if it has a dusting of snow on the hills, an illusion created by the chalk which is never far from the surface. The track swings round to the left by a small conifer plantation, then right at the end of the wood **C**. The other track on the left leads down to the Ridgeway youth hostel at Court Hill. The hostel itself is part of a complex created out of a group of old barns, brought to the site, which now together form the Ridgeway Centre for field studies **19**. The way continues as a broad green track through very open downland, an area where there is a good chance of seeing hares, especially in spring when the males can often be seen engaging in 'boxing matches' or behaving like the proverbial mad March hare. The patches of woodland are also home to deer, which regularly wander into the fields to browse, often in quite large groups. Where the track divides **D,** take the track to the left, and this is another very attractive section, where the scenery is dominated by sinuous curves, defining the shapes of the hills as plantations follow the contours and paths wind across the land.

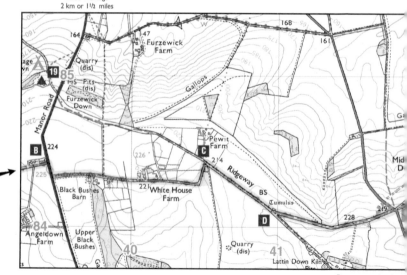

Contours are given in me
The vertical interval is

Continue straight across the B-road that heads down to Wantage, which is now visible on the valley floor. It is an attractive market town, the reputed birthplace of Alfred the Great, and home to the excellent Vale and Downland Museum. It is a little far off the route for a casual stop, but those who use it for an overnight will find much to enjoy. The land to the south is now more heavily wooded, and an attractive house can be seen nestling down in a cosy clearing. Down to the left are the remains of Grim's Ditch, not a defensive work, as the bank is too low and the ditch too shallow to prove effective. It is probably an Iron Age boundary. A far more prominent feature appears up ahead, the monument to Baron Wantage (1832–1901) **20**. It consists of a cross on a marble column, mounted on a Bronze Age barrow, and from the inscription it is clear that as a young man he served in the Crimea, taking part in the Battles of Alma and Inkerman in 1854. He is better known locally for developing the large Lockinge estate.

No one can complain of a lack of significant features along this stretch of the trail, and one of the most striking, visible for many miles, is Didcot power station with its array of immense cooling towers, which, in cold weather, create their own cloud system from the condensing steam. Some may think of it as an intrusion into the landscape, while for others the contrast between the angularity of the main buildings and the soaring curves of the towers gives it something of the quality of abstract sculpture.

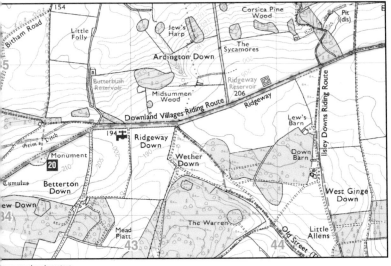

:ours are given in metres
e vertical interval is 5m

The monument to Baron Wantage, who served in the Crimean War, provides a superb vantage point for enjoying the surrounding scenery.

Beyond the Wantage monument, the landscape is increasingly marked by its small woods, all part of the Lockinge estate, their often formal shapes distinguishing them as part of a planned system of plantations. Where a track turns off to the left, continue straight on to a long line of conifers on the horizon. This is another very open section, with huge vistas, especially to the north where there is an uninterrupted view all the way past Abingdon to the outskirts of Oxford. The broad track heads up the hill towards the clump of trees on Cuckhamsley Hill, with a mound in the middle known as Scutchamer Knob **21**. Various theories have been put forward to explain the curious name. The most likely is that it derives from the name of the Saxon king Cwicchelm, who is reputed to have been buried here. The mound itself is a typical round barrow – and the

rumour that it was a king's grave would have been quite suffi-
cient for treasure hunters to break into it. An alternative sug-
gestion is that the name derives from the linen industry, where
flax was 'scutched' – beaten to break down the fibres. As the
flax was first soaked in a stream to loosen the fibres and scutch-
ing was normally carried out in small water-powered mills,
there seems no reason for anyone to bring the material away
from the water and up to the top of a hill. This theory seems
wholly improbable and the true origin may never be known.
You can while away the time thinking up your own ideas as to
who or what Scutchamer might have been.

At the top of the road to East Hendred continue straight on
along the track. The view to the north is dominated by the
Harwell Scientific Research Centre, the more recently established International Business Centre and a solitary wind tur-
bine, while up ahead the Chiltern Hills rise on the horizon.
Nearer at hand, the now familiar gallops run close by the track
and a new windbreak has been planted, consisting of rows of
trees as regular as guardsmen on parade. The way flattens out

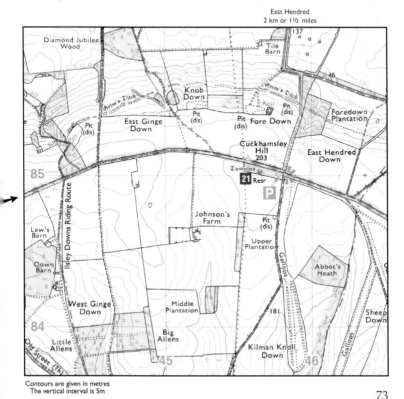

Contours are given in metres
The vertical interval is 5m

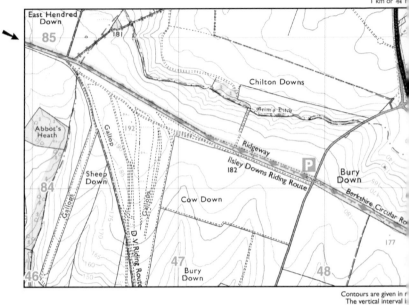

Contours are given in r
The vertical interval i

to reach the car parking area by the minor road to West Ilsley at Bury Down. In its day, this area was famous for the huge flocks of sheep roaming the hills, though these days West Ilsley itself is better known for its racing stables. Far away to the north are two prominent groups of trees, known as the Wittenham Clumps, which stand above the Thames opposite Dorchester. It is a mark of just how wayward the Thames is that our walk is now actually heading towards a crossing of the river. The route continues on a wide grass track across the minor road down to West Ilsley; once across the road there are also two tracks off the main route which also lead down to the village, so that anyone planning a visit has no shortage of options. Soon the busy traffic on the A34(T) comes into sight and earshot. Now the track starts to run downhill between fences to pass under the main road via a concrete tunnel **22**. What could have been left as a convenient, but dull, feature has been enlivened by a mural showing aspects of life in the area from Neolithic to more recent times. The section showing drovers and their sheep is accompanied by a poem:

> *Ilsley remote amid the Berkshire Downs*
> *Claims three distinctions o'er her sister towns*
> *Far famed for sheep and wool tho' not for spinners,*
> *For sportsmen, doctors, publicans and sinners.*

Emerging from the tunnel by a small copse with a communication mast, the pleasant green track gives way to the more familiar chalk track. There is a memorial stone to the left to Lieutenant Hugh Frederick Grosvenor who died here in an armoured car accident. For a time, the view to the south is closed off by a small wood, but where that comes to an end you can look across over Sheep Down to East Ilsley **23**. This is the important market town mentioned in the poem, and there is more information about this and the sheep fairs in the short

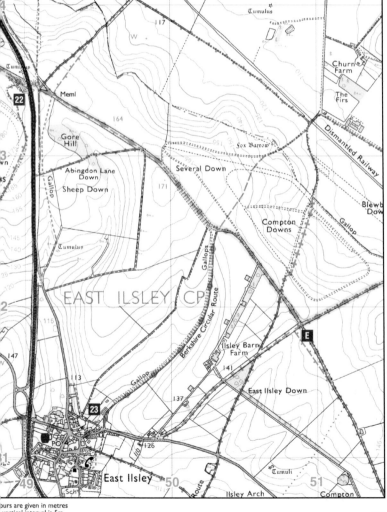

ours are given in metres
vertical interval is 5m

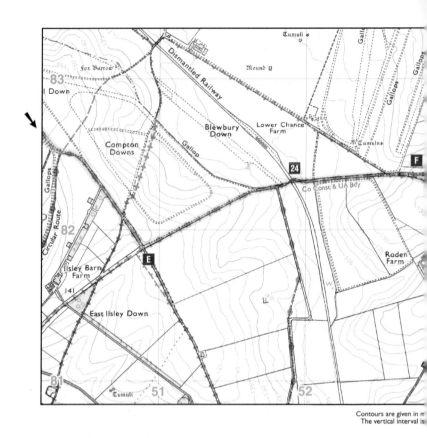

Contours are given in m
The vertical interval is

article on page 82. As the track climbs gently, it becomes grassier again. There is an interesting contrast, in that although the wider vistas remain comparatively unchanged, closer at hand one can either look at the extensive pig farm or to grassland where skylarks rise and sing. Where ways cross, carry straight on, and those wishing to visit East Ilsley can take the track on the right.

On reaching the long line of trees stretching away to the south, the rough track gives way to a road, and we are again in racing country with gallops and hurdles alongside the trail. Cross straight on over the first track junction, but at the next one, leave the surfaced road and turn left **E.** This goes steadily downhill but, as can all too clearly be seen, it will soon be climbing back up again. The open views continue, and over to the left there are obvious bumps on the hillside, which even from a distance have the appearance of barrows, though only one, Fox Barrow, is positively identified, the remainder simply lumped together as tumuli. (This is the term used by the correctly cautious Ordnance Survey, where a mound's origins can be guessed at but not actually proved.) A bridleway on the right leads down to Compton, but the route ahead continues over a slight hump, which turns out to be a bridge over a disused railway cutting **24**.

This is the track of the former Didcot, Newbury and Southampton Junction Railway, a company whose performance never quite lived up to the grandeur of its name, though it became important for a while in the Second World War, when some sections of the old single line were doubled. Begun in 1882, it failed to celebrate its centenary, being closed in 1962.

New hedgerows have been planted along the next length of the Ridgeway, and the track ahead appears as two parallel routes also divided by hawthorn hedges. This is a gentle hill and just before reaching the top, where the way divides **F**, take the track on the right where new hedgerows have been planted. At the top everything opens out to a vista of very pleasant grassland, where a few deciduous trees have been

Much of the grazing land of the Downs has now been ploughed.

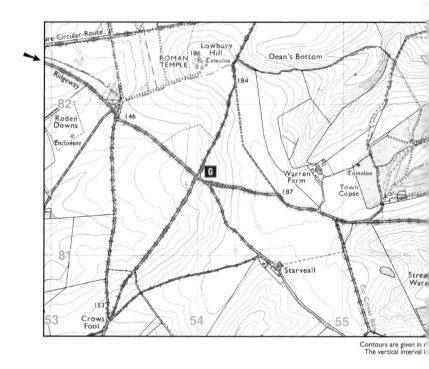

Contours are given in r
The vertical interval i

planted. In contrast, a clump of pine appears up ahead, an unusual intrusion into this landscape. Over to the left is beautifully, softly curved Lowbury Hill, which the map shows as the site of a Roman temple, though nothing is visible from the trail. To the right, down in the valley, is the very attractive group of red-brick buildings of Roden Farm that seems almost big enough to be a hamlet.

At a complex track-crossing continue straight on by an area of scrubby woodland, and now the views are temporarily lost as hedgerows appear on either side. Here there is one of those little, winding woodland paths running parallel to the wide track on the left. Carry straight on at the next track-crossing, and just beyond that, at a little triangle of woodland **G**, take the path to the left. This is the last short climb of this section of the walk, up a chalk path, with nodules of flint shining through.

Once the hedges end at the left, there is a particularly fine view over hillsides, covered in a woodland patchwork, and the Ridgeway begins to lose something of its downland character and take on more of the qualities of the richer Thames valley. The grassland is now able to support cattle as well as sheep,

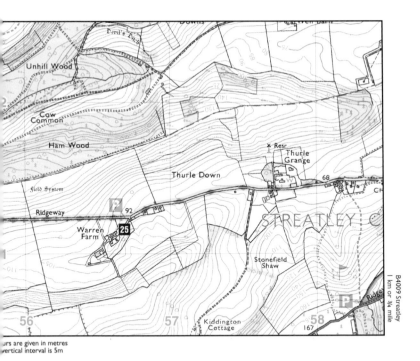

…urs are given in metres
…vertical interval is 5m

and farms appear with greater regularity. Sheep farms invariably require a far greater acreage to support their flocks on the short upland grass than do dairy farms for their herds in the lusher pastures of the valley. The Ridgeway is also entering a section where it is worth looking up as well as around, for this is an area much favoured by birds of prey. You may spot a hovering kestrel, glimpse a marauding sparrowhawk or, most spectacularly, see a soaring red kite, though the latter will be much more common further along the way. These big birds seem quite unconcerned by passing walkers: if anything they seem rather curious to see what's going on and will come over for a better look.

Once the view opens out to the right, it brings one of those surprising stretches of countryside that make the Ridgeway such a delight. One becomes very accustomed to the wide vistas, but here a deep, steep-sided valley suddenly falls away to the south of the path. Smooth sided, its headland planted with a small copse, this is Streatley Warren – a name which goes some way to explaining the appearance of so many raptors in search of a rabbit dinner. The track heads straight on towards the farm at the foot of the valley **25**, with a magnificent collection of buildings,

From Lardon Chase, the Ridgeway dips steeply down to cross the Thames at Goring.

constructed in a rich, red brick which would have been fired from local clay, so that the whole array looks totally at home in the landscape. The tiled roofs have been given an orange patina by lichens. This marks the start of a quiet country road leading down to Streatley. More houses soon appear, showing other aspects of vernacular building, with thatched roofs alongside tile, and timber framing beside brick, all combining in a most satisfactory way to mark the end of this beautiful little valley. All the way down the lane there is a scattering of houses interspersed with grassland, broken up by copses and hedgerows. There is one very grand house, Thurle Grange, approached down an avenue of tall, clipped yew, and a golf course before the lane emerges at the main road **H**. Turn right to walk into Streatley.

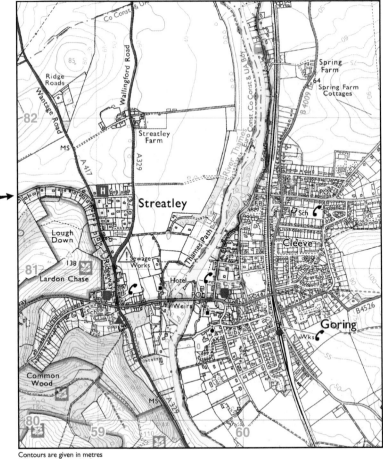

Contours are given in metres
The vertical interval is 5m

Sheep and sheep fairs

It is hard to over-value the important place that sheep held in the British economy until quite modern times. It has been estimated that in 1500 the human population of England was no more than 3 million – but there were 8 million sheep. Wool was needed for everything from blankets to clothes, and only the very rich could afford such expensive alternatives as linen or silk. By the beginning of the 18th century, commentators such as Daniel Defoe were still praising the virtues of wool and its importance to the British people: 'Heaven bestow'd the wool upon them, the life and soul, the original of all their commerce; he gave it to them, and have it exclusively of all the nations in the world, for none comes up to it.' But already in Defoe's time a competitor had appeared from overseas, cotton, and the downlands themselves were changing. In his great survey of the country which he published in 1724–26, Defoe reported that the downs 'were formerly all left open to be fed by the large flocks of sheep so often mentioned; but now so much of these downs are plowed up, as has increased the quantity of corn produced in this county [Wiltshire] in a prodigious manner, and lessened their quantity of wool.' The sheep were no longer roaming free, but were being gathered into folds at night, and were moved on the next day.

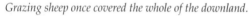

Grazing sheep once covered the whole of the downland.

They enriched the poor soil with their droppings and hastened the move from pasture to arable. It is a process that continues today, when more and more of the uplands has been put to the plough. Even so, Defoe was able to describe sheep fairs, where he was told that as many as 500,000 sheep might be sold at a single fair in Wiltshire – though he was a good enough reporter to doubt the accuracy of the figures. Nevertheless, it is clear that the downs supported immense flocks.

The sheep have played an important role in both the history and appearance of the downland. Once the land was cleared of trees, their steady munching prevented the woodlands from returning. The grassland flourished and there are few more comfortable surfaces for walkers than the short, soft grass of the downs. The unimproved grassland is particularly rich in plant species of all kinds, including orchids, and can often be seen at its best in a number of nature reserves to be met along the trail. The woodlands also had their part to play in this sheepish story. Twigs were woven together to make the light hurdles of wattle for temporary pens, both on arable land and at the sheep fairs. These fairs played a vital role in the life of the local communities. East Ilsley **23** lies just south of the Ridgeway, surrounded by a web of roads and tracks down which the flocks were driven to sheep fairs, which have been held here since medieval times. However, it only received its official market charter in 1620, thanks to the influence of the Lord of the Manor, Sir Francis Moore. At the height of its prosperity as many as 80,000 sheep could be brought to market in a single day. Drovers converged on the village from a wide area, coming from as far away as Salisbury Plain, and driving was a thirsty business, which no doubt explains why the village could support more than a dozen pubs. Those times have gone, and most of the pubs as well, but The Crown and Horns still has much of the atmosphere of an old market pub. The surrounding downland has changed as well, for it is now home to more expensive animals – the racehorses that work out on the numerous gallops. The last major sheep fair was held in 1934 and, in spite of a few attempts to revive the tradition, those days are unlikely ever to return. The market for wool has all but vanished, and modern taste calls for lamb not mutton – even if there are still some who would welcome the stronger flavour of the older beasts. It is doubtful if anyone again will be able to stand on the downs as Daniel Defoe did, and be told that there were 600,000 sheep grazing within a 6-mile radius of that spot.

Alfred's kingdom

The wealth of prehistoric sites met along the Ridgeway can easily lead one to overlook the fact that the walk passes through the heart of one of the great kingdoms of the Dark Ages. In AD 825 Egbert of Wessex won a victory over the reigning Mercian ruler and established a new dynasty of West Saxons. His grandson, Alfred, was born in Wantage in 849, taking the throne in 871. Thanks to his famous victory over the Danes, he was to be known as Alfred the Great. Wantage itself was a royal manor until 1199, and the town's most famous son is remembered in a suitably martial statue in the market square. Local tradition has it that the famous white horse, carved on the hillside 6 miles (10 km) to the west of Wantage, commemorates Alfred's great victory of 871. This is now thought to be very unlikely, but as yet no one has been able to provide an accurate date for the figure. Even if the Alfred version is untrue, it shows how his life has become intertwined with legend.

Alfred was far more than a winner of battles: he was also determined to consolidate his kingdom. He organised a series of fortified towns, known as *burhs*. There were 31 of them in all, so distributed that no one within Wessex was more than 25 miles from a fortified centre. One of the best preserved examples was created at an important Thames crossing, Wallingford. The first written description comes in the *Burghal Hidage* of circa 919. This lists all the *burhs* in terms of their size measured in *hides*. This does not seem to have been a very accurate measurement, but was defined as the amount of land needed to support one family. It also specified the number of men required to defend the settlement, based on the number of hides. Wallingford was listed as having 2,400 hides, and each hide was to supply one man for defence, and four men were needed to cover one pole of the walls. Translating this into modern units would give a perimeter wall of 9,900 feet (3,017 metres). Wallingford today still has much of its defensive wall intact. One side of the town was defined by the Thames, and the other three sides by defensive banks. By adding the length of wall to the river frontage, the result tallies very closely with the formula spelled out in the 10th century. Within the walls, the town was laid out with a regular grid of streets, so that it looks remarkably like a Roman town in its overall pattern. This was an important place in Saxon times, with its own mint. Wallingford's Saxon lord Wigod was a supporter of William the Conqueror, which did no harm to the town's status,

Alfred the Great looks imperiously down over Wantage, where he was born more than a thousand years ago.

and in 1067 the Normans built a castle to control this important river crossing. The shape of the old town remains clear. Parts of the town walls have survived as banks, but archaeologists have found post holes suggesting that the walls might once have been topped with a palisade. The cross of main streets is still clear, with one main street running up from the old bridge. The earliest record of a bridge dates back to 1141, though the name Walling*ford* suggests that the town lived without one for a long time. Remnants of the old medieval bridge survive, but it was mostly rebuilt in 1809. There is a chance to visit this fascinating town by means of a circular walk (page 100).

The consolidation of the Kingdom of Wessex depended on good transport as much as on fortified towns. Roads were vital links for moving armies as well as for trade. This was officially recognised in the decades before the Norman Conquest, when four routes were placed under royal protection: two of them were the Ridgeway and the Icknield Way. So one can take a pride in the fact that this walk not only takes you along an ancient track, but is one which, if only briefly, enjoyed royal status.

4 Streatley to Watlington Hill Road

via North Stoke and Swyncombe
15 miles (24 km)

On reaching the main road, there is a first glimpse of the Thames, and an introduction to Streatley. There is a marked contrast between the new development on the left and the traditional houses of the region on the right. Place Manor boasts a complex of roofs, which seem to defy all building logic but combine to produce a wonderfully picturesque effect. By the traffic lights, there is a fine example of just what makes Georgian architecture so enduringly appealing, and why modern attempts to copy it so often miss the point. It is all about proportion, and the discreet use of classical motifs. Just look, for example, at the little urns added as an embellishment to the door frame – very understated, simply offering a hint that the builder understood he was following a classical tradition. Urns appear on the new houses opposite, but blown up to grotesque size, in the middle of a swirling broken pediment. The size might just about be right for the grandest of country houses. This group at the crossroads also contains the attractive Bull Inn **26**.

Turn left at the traffic lights and yet more splendid buildings appear in a variety of local styles, happily mixing the thatched cottage with Georgian elegance. It seems likely that a local builder was responsible for more than one 18th-century house, as the urn motif reappears on another doorway of a particularly grand example. The church, which was largely rebuilt in the late 19th century, can be seen over to the left. The road now leads down to the bridge over the Thames, where the Ridgeway shares a short section of road with another National Trail, the Thames Path. Here there is a complex system of weirs to control the flow **27**. The Thames was a major trading route from prehistory until quite recently, but its present appearance dates back to changes introduced in the 18th century through the system of weirs and locks. The weirs allow the river to flow, controlled by sluices, regardless of the passage of boats. The weirs also act as dams, building a good head of water on the upstream side. Artificial cuttings were then dug, containing a lock, so that boats no longer had to plunge downhill, but could move in a controlled manner. Before the arrival of the lock, boats going downstream had to wait until there was a head of water above the weir, then sluice gates were opened and the boats rode the flood through the gates – an alarming experience. In 1634 a passenger boat was shooting the weir on the Goring side when it overturned and 60 people lost their lives. Looking at the weir today, it is difficult to believe that such boats ever undertook such a perilous journey. On a happier note, the river is graced by an ornate former college barge. At the far end of the bridge, there is a quiet backwater with boathouses, whose original use will soon be made clear.

Crossing the bridge takes us from Streatley to neighbouring Goring, and down to the right of the road is the former Goring Mill. Here it is still easy to see where the waterwheel originally turned, and the weather-boarded sack hoist rises alongside the wheel pit. Once across the bridge, turn left up Thames Road **A**, passing modern developments. At the end of the road continue straight on along the narrow path between hedges, still urban but with glimpses of the river down below. Reaching the road again, turn left. Looking over to the right at the first road junction, there is a bridge carrying the railway. This is a reminder that this section of the walk is going through the so-called Goring Gap, where the river has eaten its way through the chalk ridge and the different transport routes of river, road and railway are all squeezed together. Meanwhile, the Ridgeway has

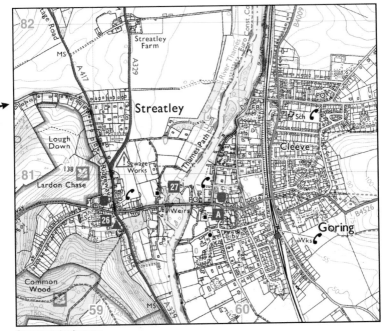

Contours are given in metres
The vertical interval is 5m

combined with a long-distance riding route, Swan's Way. Where the houses end on the right, there is an open space containing a deep cutting, created in the early 19th century for the main line of Brunel's Great Western Railway. There are still reminders of the days when the GWR controlled the land close to the railway in the shape of a pair of cast-iron gateposts by A. and J. Main of Glasgow, London and Dublin. The route continues as a bridleway with the railway on one side and views down to the river on the other. Where this comes to an end, continue on the roadway opposite signed as 'Private Road No Entry', an instruction that quite definitely does not apply to walkers or riders. This takes you past a boat club and a number of very large houses. One of the houses is called The Bridleway, acknowledging that the existing route was also there before this was a private road, while another, Cedar Cottage, looks to a later transport addition to the landscape and has its house name in the form of a small-scale locomotive name plate.

Where the houses end, the railway exerts its influence as a high embankment. This is a common feature of railway engineering, where the spoil excavated to create a cutting is piled up to build a bank across the neighbouring valley. The path now runs out in the open, past a reed bed and over a common towards South Stoke. Walk straight on along the road through this attractive village, which boasts an enormous and imposing old vicarage and a comparatively modest church. The latter is typical of the area, with flint walls and a square tower. A visit to the church **28** reveals that at least one of the incumbents was a man of considerable importance. There is a funerary monument in the chancel to Dr Griffith Higgs, born 1589 and at one time Chaplain to the Queen of Bohemia. His carved portrait stands above a lengthy Latin inscription, listing his good works – no wonder the church had such a grand vicarage. At the end of the street, turn left past the Corner House, an old timber-framed building, jettied out over the road. Where the road turns sharply right, go left **B** on the path down to the river. Reaching the river, turn right onto the riverside footpath, bordered by extensive beds of reeds, bullrushes and tussocky grass. On the far side there are the grand houses of Moulsford, with gardens leading down to the water's edge.

The path passes beneath the railway viaduct **29**, which is an unusual and interesting structure. On first approach one is struck by the shapely, low arches, but on closer inspection they appear as quite complex structures. The line crosses the river at

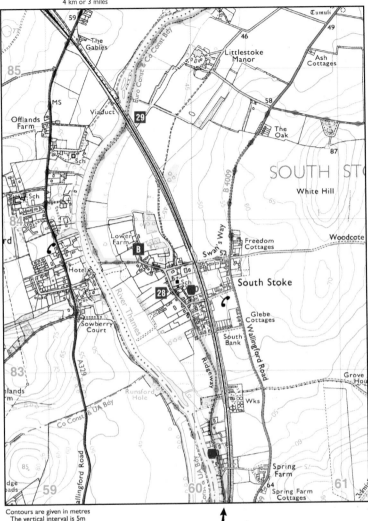

Contours are given in metres
The vertical interval is 5m

an angle, so the viaduct was built on the skew, which meant the bricks had to be laid in diagonal courses, as you can see from the dog-tooth pattern created at the sides of the arches. Then, more surprisingly, this is not one viaduct, but two built side by side, to take increased traffic. The original, round stone piers can still be seen. The path now continues along the riverside grassland, which seems to be a popular gathering point for Canada geese, which now outnumber the traditional population of mallard, swan, moorhen and grebe that can be found on the water. Littlestoke Manor can be seen over to the right, with an immense barn, which seems to be even bigger than the house. A tributary stream is crossed by a simple bridge, beside which is an old Second World War pillbox. Here the path turns right and immediately left to continue a little further from the water's edge.

On the approach to North Stoke, a drainage ditch is crossed by a little cast-iron bridge topped by concrete. The path continues through a kissing-gate to enter the churchyard. Outwardly the church **30** is very similar to that of neighbouring South Stoke, but there is a surprise waiting inside. The walls are covered by medieval wall paintings, dating back to the 14th century. Inevitably they have faded over the years, and parts have been lost, but it is still possible to make out such familiar Biblical scenes as *The Last Supper* and *The Last Judgement*. What is so interesting about such paintings is the way in which the different characters are all shown as English, in the manner and costume of the time in which they were painted. It is not too difficult to imagine these same people occupying these pews some 600 years ago. Leave the church by the lych-gate, continue up to the road and turn left, passing an attractive little village hall of 1911. Just beyond that is an old water mill, easily identified by the rather worn millstone propped up outside. There is also quite a large pond, fed by a long leat from the Thames, which would have served the mill. The route continues past a golf course and follows a track, lined with some majestic beech trees, which eventually becomes a very pleasant grassy path. The golf course is soon replaced by formal parkland, with a typically sparse scattering of impressive trees, with the oaks the grandest of all. To the left is a small wood, with areas of reedy pools, which is a private nature reserve.

The path continues through the buildings of what was until recently Carmel College. Where the walk known as Judge's Ride goes off to the right, carry straight on past the lake on the right, home to a large number of water fowl and other birds, such as wagtails, which spend most of their time near water. Like the pond at North Stoke, this too is fed by a leat from the Thames, and here too there is what is almost certainly another former mill. The road turns round to the right, but the trail goes straight on along the paved path. On reaching the main road **C** turn right. The circular walk round Wallingford (page 100) begins here and goes through the tunnel under the road. The path continues alongside the road, goes through a kissing-gate, and then wanders along through a thin patch of woodland. It passes the far end of the lake first met by the college and arrives at a busy main road, which unfortunately does not enjoy the benefit of an underpass. Cross over with care as there is a lot of fast moving traffic. At the far side, turn right and immediately left.

The next section of the walk is very enjoyable, a little wandering path with a screen of trees and fields stretching away on either side. It is also very intriguing. There is a short climb and

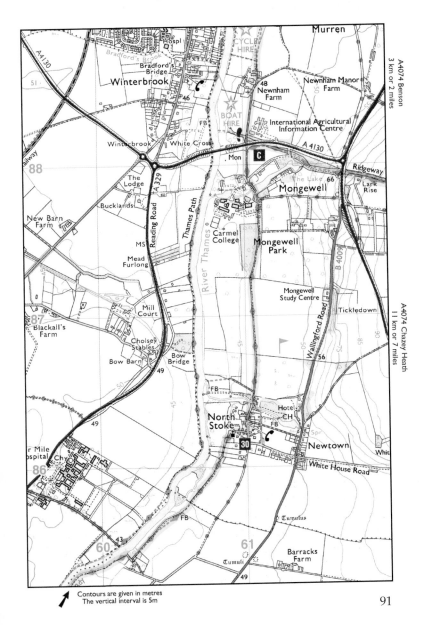

Contours are given in metres
The vertical interval is 5m

then the path emerges on the top of what is clearly a man-made bank. It is known as Grim's Ditch, and may or may not be associated with the Grim's Ditch encountered briefly earlier on in the walk (page 71). Archaeologists are uncertain whether they were indeed once connected, and they are equally unsure as to just when it was constructed. The likeliest date is some time in the Iron Age, but everyone seems to be agreed that it could never have been used for defence. It would seem, therefore, that it represents some form of boundary between different territories, and that would appear to be about all that can be said with any certainty. As the name would have been given several centuries after construction, it has no real significance. But this is definitely a very important landscape feature, which runs for 5 miles (8 km) from the bank of the Thames to end at the foot of the Chilterns. In the latter part it will become far more dramatic.

One good reason for travelling the Ridgeway in spring is to enjoy the bluebells that carpet much of the woodland along the way.

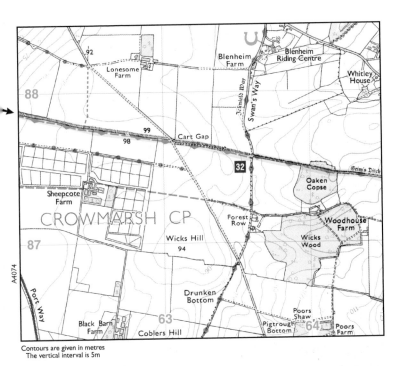

Contours are given in metres
The vertical interval is 5m

This part of the walk produces the effect of a stroll along a raised path through a narrow wood. It feels as if it is all on the flat, yet there is a trig. point along the way – an invitation to take advantage of a high point, however modest, to have a look around. To one side is Sheepcote Farm, which belies its name by now being a pig-rearing centre, while the solitary farm to the north is, by contrast, well suited to its name – Lonesome Farm. Coming down to the road, which slices through the bank, provides the wider vista of tree-topped hills. Cross straight over the road to continue following the path on the bank, which is even more well-defined than before. Another road soon appears, this time on the course of the Icknield Way **32**. This was, like the Ridgeway itself, originally a prehistoric track, running all the way from the Thames to the north coast of Norfolk. Crossing straight over this other ancient route, the path now begins a gentle climb heading to woodland which, although called Oaken Copse, is now very mixed with a large proportion given over to conifers, and the remainder mostly birch and beech. The path leaves the top of the bank, though still continuing alongside it. The woodland itself is very attractive, particularly in spring when the bluebells are in flower.

This attractive wooded path runs along the edge of Grim's Ditch, an impressive but mysterious feature in the landscape.

Leaving the wood behind, the sweeping curves in the valley and the hills topped by woodland provide the sort of scene that has appealed to generations of English landscape painters. As the path begins to climb, Grim's Ditch becomes just that, a deep depression by the side of the walk. It was obviously much more sensible to mark the boundary by digging a ditch in the rising ground than it was to pile up earthworks to create the bank. Over the years, the ditch must have been partially filled in and trees have grown in the hollow. Some have fallen over, and the exposed roots show just how shallow the soil layer is above the chalk. The next section of the walk is not just attractive but a complete contrast to most of what has gone before. It is contained within a broad strip of beechwood, undulates and winds and has the immense ditch as a constant accompaniment. The path occasionally changes sides, but never strays far from the ditch. At the top of the hill, the path becomes stony so that roots spread out over the surface, hardened and polished by the passing of countless walkers. This is a most beautiful section, which has all the benefits of mature woodland while at the same time offering wide and constantly changing views. A solitary house appears beside the path, with a water tap alongside it. From here the path runs on the outside of the wood for a while, offering a view out towards Oxford, with Didcot power station by now a very familiar landmark.

The end of the wood **D** also marks the end of Grim's Ditch, and the path turns left towards Nuffield. The trail now continues down beside a hedge to the road and a right turn into Nuffield village. The church **33** is ancient and occupies the site of a Roman villa. Some of the Roman tiles were incorporated into the structure and are easily recognised as long, narrow dusty red inserts into the flint. There are some on the north wall, and rather more round the top of the tower. The oldest part is the present nave, to which the side aisle and tower are 'modern' additions, hardly 1,000 years old. The interior has been sadly restored by heavy-handed Victorians. This is a pleasant spot to pause, and there is even a water tap kindly provided for refreshment. Just beyond the church, turn left onto the footpath heading diagonally across the field to the golf clubhouse.

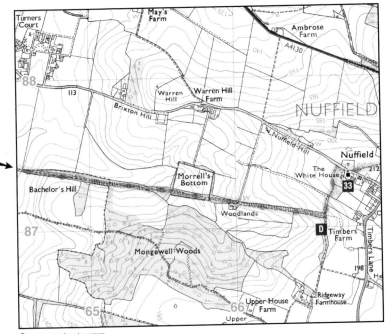

Contours are given in metres
The vertical interval is 5m

The path now crosses the course, the route marked by numbered posts. There is a brief excursion into a patch of woodland before the next bit of the course appears and there are more numbers to follow. The approach to the road looks unlikely, but really does go down the gravel drive in front of the houses. Cross over the busy main road, which carries a good deal of fast traffic, to take the kissing-gate into the wood. There is a very obvious path heading diagonally down the hill, through comparatively young trees which are being enhanced by recently planted saplings. At the edge of the wood, the path across the next field is waymarked by a white post at the edge of the woods opposite. Once through the narrow strip of woodland, the way is once again shown by a post, just visible in the distance. The field is deceptively large – and deceptively steep – but it eventually ends at another little wood.

At the end of this wood, at a track junction **E**, turn right on a track through the Ewelme Park estate; the house itself soon appears **34**. It is very grand, though not very old. The inspiration is largely Tudor, but the details and use of local materials recall architects such as Charles Voysey who developed a distinctive English country house style at the end of the 19th century. Today, the estate is used for a range of educational visits. Walkers are likely to be greeted by barking dogs and to come under the scrutiny of a crowd of peacocks and peahens. The track continues through the barns, then turns right as a double track, and the Ridgeway stays to the right-hand side along the avenue of trees, then continues between hedgerows. It turns down to the left for a steep descent through woodland to emerge in formal parkland. At the bottom of the field, go through a kissing-gate **F** and turn right. The path runs alongside a fence, protecting the estate of Swyncombe House, and there are tantalising glimpses of the tops of ornamental trees. This arrives at the church **35,** famous in the early part of the year for its displays of snowdrops. Each church met on this section of the walk has its own distinctive features. This one reflects the wealth and importance of the owners of Swyncombe House, with gilded roof bosses and heraldic devices in the windows. There is also a curious modern window, featuring an RAF biplane above a traditional scene of a hayfield with working horses. A 20th-century rood screen stands in front of the semicircular Norman apse. The Saxon builders of the first church on this site would probably be astonished at how it has been elaborated through the centuries. The road passes the old rectory, which again reflects the wealth of the patrons, for it is a very large house serving a small church and a scattered community.

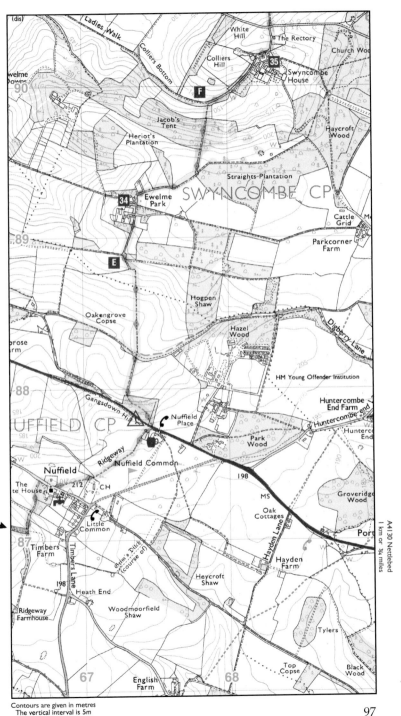

Contours are given in metres
The vertical interval is 5m

The red kite now thrives in the Chilterns after a long absence.

At the T-junction carry straight on across the road and take the gate on the right for the path that dips and then climbs the hill towards the wood. Once again, these wooded hills prove a popular hunting ground for birds of prey, with buzzards seeming quite happy to share the space with the increasingly familiar red kite. Until recently these beautiful birds were to be found only in Mid Wales, but once reintroduced to the Chilterns they thrived and are now comparatively common. They can be distinguished by their forked tails and red undersides. The path continues to the top of the hill and then proceeds to go just as steeply down again, staying at first in the wood, which ends at one of those smoothly scooped out valleys which are among the visual delights of the Chilterns.

At the farm buildings **G**, turn right and cross straight over the minor road to Britwell Salome, a name which disappointingly has nothing to do with the famous lady of the seven veils. For the first time for several miles, the track is now a byway, but a restricted byway, which means that it is closed to recreational vehicles. After 300 yards walkers will also be able to leave the main track for another of those little footpaths through the trees. At a meeting of tracks, carry straight on down the minor, surface road or take a permissive path to the side of it. This section ends at the B-road by a field amicably shared between sheep, geese and hens. This is the start of a circular walk to Christmas Common (page 102). Cross straight over to the track opposite, which ends at the minor road down into Watlington.

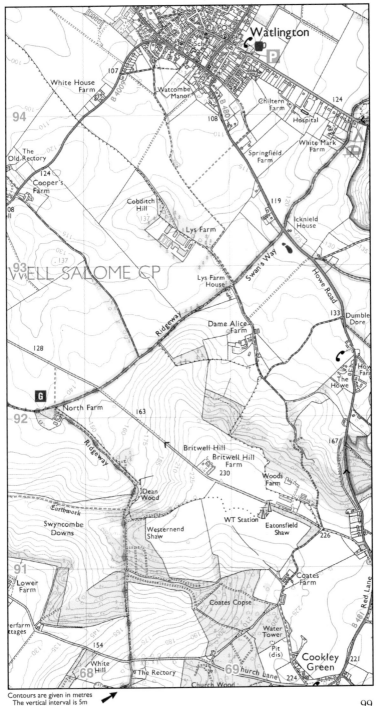

Contours are given in metres
The vertical interval is 5m

A Walk round Wallingford

3 ½ miles (5.5 km)

Wallingford is a town of considerable historic interest, and can be reached and explored by this comparatively short excursion from the main route. The town could well be used as a stopping-off point during the walk. Where the Ridgeway turns right, just before reaching the A4130, carry straight on along the bridleway and through the underpass. At the edge of the caravan park, turn left across the field to the end of the bridge and join the road **AA**. The multi-arched bridge has been much altered over the centuries: some of the present structure might date back to the 13th century, but it was very largely reconstructed in 1809. Cross over the bridge, which provides a fine view of a number of handsome town houses and a converted wharf building. The walk continues straight up the High Street, which has a fascinating mixture of buildings, the oldest of which date back to the 16th century. These can easily be recognised by the way in which they are 'jettied', with the upper floors protruding out over the pavement. Other outstanding buildings are the splendid Cavella House, dating from the early 18th century, and The George Inn, built around a courtyard. Turn left down St Mary's Street, which brings you into the Market Square overlooked by the elegant Town Hall of 1670.

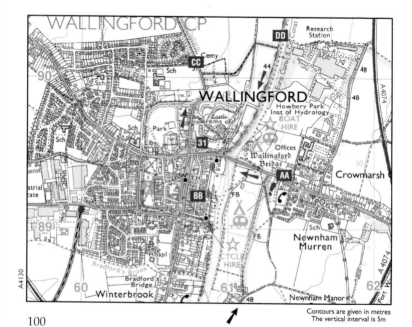

Contours are given in metres
The vertical interval is 5m

Wallingford's ancient bridge was rebuilt in the 18th century.

A curious feature is an ornate cast-iron fountain: not too surprising, however, if you know that there was once a foundry just a short distance away. At the square **BB**, double back on the road parallel to St Mary's Street, and cross over the next road. On the right is the entrance to the Castle Gardens **31**.

There is little of the castle remaining, largely because Wallingford backed the losing side in the Civil War. The most prominent feature is the huge motte or mound on which the scant remains of the keep can be seen. Rather more obvious are the immense earthworks, but there is more to these than at first appears. Long before the Norman invasion, Wallingford was one of the *burhs*, Saxon fortified towns established by King Alfred in the 9th century as protection against the Danes (page 84). The entire town was surrounded by earthworks, parts of which were incorporated into the Norman defences.

Leave the park, return to the road and turn right, continuing until you reach a path that runs between the old and new sections of the cemetery **CC**. Once past the end of the wall, with its attractive flint inlays, turn right onto the grassland. Now the shape and size of the old Saxon defences becomes very clear. Follow the footpath, which swings away to the left, then turns right to a gate. Once through the gate, continue down to the river bank and turn right on to the Thames Path **DD**. On the opposite bank is a small boathouse, with a fetching spiral staircase leading to the landing stage. Continue on the path back to the bridge, which can now be seen rather more clearly. It is very much of its period, with a wide navigation arch, and the whole enlivened by pilasters and a balustrade. Cross back over the bridge and return to the start.

A Circular Walk via Christmas Common
5 ¹/₂ miles (9 km)

This is a walk for all those who would like an opportunity to spend more time exploring the beautiful beech woods of the Chilterns. The walk starts at the point where the Ridgeway meets the B-road **AA**. Turn right up the road and, after a short way, turn left on the track with a sign to Lower Dean and continue on the broad track running in front of the houses. It goes steadily uphill to the woodland, then turns left to follow the edge of the wood. The grassland to the left appears to be a regular hunting ground for red kite. Once past the buildings of Little Dean, the track becomes a pleasant green footpath that swings off into the wood for the final climb to the top of the hill. On reaching the road **BB** turn right, then right again at the road junction towards Christmas Common. Just before reaching the village turn left down the road and after a short way take the obvious track off to the right. The broad, sunken track leads into Queen and College Wood, mixed woodland but inevitably dominated by beech. As the track leaves the wood, the view opens out to yet more wooded hills. The track levels out and heads towards a farm. Just before reaching it **CC** turn right by a stile and take the path beside the fence towards the wood. Cross the stile to enter the wood and carry straight on. Where the path divides, take the route to the right, heading down into the valley, through this very attractive woodland. At the clearing at the

The wood anemone thrives in the Chiltern beechwoods.

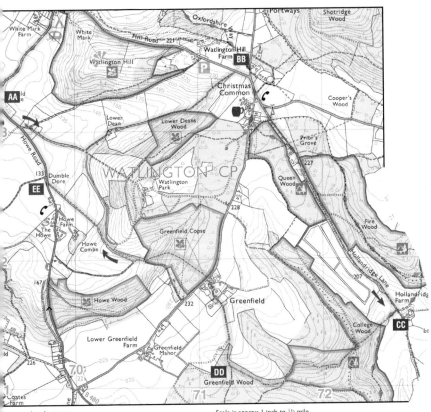

ours are given in metres
vertical interval is 5m

Scale is approx 1 inch to ¹/₂ mile

foot of the hill, take the path on the left past a large holly tree, with an arrow marked W21. The path now climbs up the other side of the valley, and having reached the top swings round to the left and goes back down again. At the bottom, where tracks meet **DD**, turn right on to the path waymarked as W19. The track soon emerges at open farmland and continues on towards the houses, and between them to reach the road.

Cross straight over the road, go through the wooden gate and carry straight on into the next patch of woodland. Where the path forks, take the route to the left, indicated by a white arrow. Continue following the path as it turns to the right, still going downhill. Cross straight over the broad track to a stile opposite and take the path heading through a thin strip of woodland. The path winds through an old coppice to reach farmland. It continues across a stile to reach a path beside the field. This leads down to the road **EE**. Turn right to return to the start.

Beechwoods are one of the dominant features of the eastern end of the Ridgeway and in

ing the bluebells appear in all their glory.

5 Watlington Hill Road to Wendover

via Princes Risborough
17 miles (27 km)

Cross over the road to take the broad track opposite, which runs at the foot of an area of scrubby woodland that soon gives way to a conifer plantation. The path is very straight, running along the foot of the Chilterns with the flatter landscape of the Oxfordshire plain to the north, and indeed the Oxfordshire Way

The Chiltern woodlands are dominated by beech and the fallen leaves and beechnuts provide a soft carpet for the walkers.

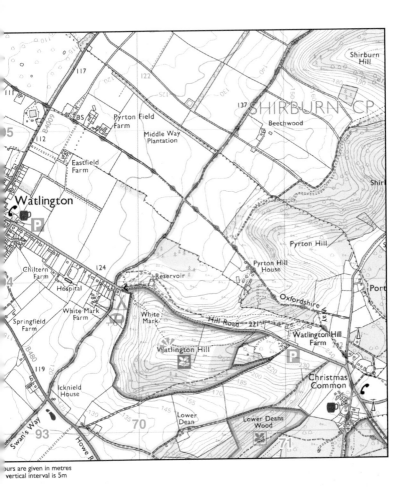

ours are given in metres
vertical interval is 5m

appears at the next track-crossing. Although the Ridgeway itself continues on its straight line, its nature varies considerably. It becomes enclosed for a time between hedgerows, then opens out to a handsome broad track running down an avenue of trees, inevitably dominated by beech. Over to the left, several of the fields have been protected by wind breaks, and one of these, Middle Way Plantation, reaches down to the walk while another runs parallel to the Ridgeway. The track now begins a long but gentle climb towards the lower slopes of shapely, wood-crowned Shirburn Hill, and through the gaps in the trees to the left there are occasional glimpses of Shirburn Castle. The scenery remains very much the same, with most of the interest concentrated on the undulating landscape to the east, dominated by Bald Hill, which in spite of its name boasts

Beneath the Chiltern escarpment, downland gives way to more fertile farming land of arable and pasture.

a significant fringe of trees. Now the track is grassy, heading off towards the M40. Hill Farm to the right must once have enjoyed a delightfully peaceful situation, but that changed for ever with the coming of the motorway, as did much else. A deep cutting was carved through the hills, which when the road was new appeared as a startlingly white gash and, though time has softened the colours, it remains a striking feature in the landscape.

An underpass takes walkers safely beyond the motorway and the route continues as another broad track, still keeping very close to the foot of the hills. The next in the line is Beacon Hill, which has an attractive array of silver birch on the lower slopes. In summer it has an extra attraction to offer. The Aston Rowant National Nature Reserve by the path **36** consists of natural chalk downland and is home to a flower peculiar to the area, the Chiltern gentian, and the equally local Chalkhill blue butterfly. Reaching an area of beechwood, the noise of the motorway is muffled and soon fades away completely. An attractive brick and flint house stands beside the once busy A40, now largely ignored by motorists who prefer the six lanes of the M40. The next section is a bridleway and is very attractive, enclosed by trees, but these are sufficiently well spaced to allow the views to be enjoyed. The artificial bank which appears to the left **37** has nothing to do with defence or ancient boundaries, but was built to carry the GWR branch line from Princes Risborough to Watlington. Although the line closed in 1957, a section near Chinnor has recently reopened as the Icknield Line, worked by both diesel and steam locomotives. What would the original users of the Icknield Way have made of that?

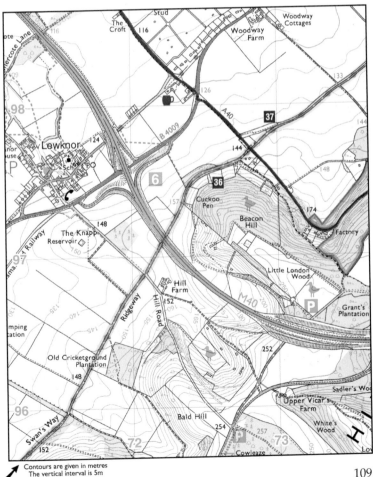

Contours are given in metres
The vertical interval is 5m

The wooded hills continue to provide an attractive backdrop, as the route crosses the minor road down to Kingston Blount. At the top of the nearest hill is the tall communication mast of Stokenchurch, while nearer at hand the Kingston racecourse appears on the right. Race meetings are not very frequent, but it must make this section very exciting when the horses are thundering past only a few yards away. The old railway now turns away towards Chinnor, a fine panoramic view opens up and a new landmark appears. This is the tall chimney of Chinnor cement works **38**, which has had a huge impact on the landscape. Chalk has been dug from shallow pits and deep quarries, which now line the route for the next mile. Since abandonment, they have filled with water and provide homes for a variety of water fowl. Walkers without binoculars may have difficulty in identifying the different species, but there is no mistaking the loud honkings of a considerable

The flowers of the chalk downs are a constant delight and few are more beautiful than the spotted orchid.

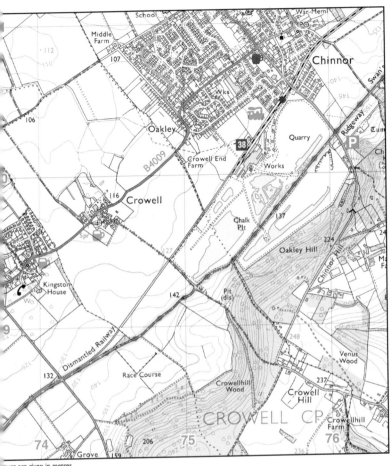

goose population. The man-made lakes might be thought an
eyesore by some, but looking down on them from the walk,
they appear very dramatic and the chalk has turned them an
astonishing turquoise blue. To the right is the Oakley Hill
Nature Reserve, once again a section of preserved downland.
This section of the Ridgeway really is a ridgeway, not in the
sense of being a natural feature, but because it has been left
isolated by the immense, deep pits to either side. Just before
reaching the road, you get a chance to see just how deep these
quarries are, as one has not yet filled with water.

Cross straight over the road, and the track is steadily climbing, providing views down to the outskirts of Chinnor. A little
further on, by the houses, a path leads down to the village. Just

A view from the Ridgeway overlooking Princes Risborough.

beyond the houses is another nature reserve, where the scrub has been thinned to allow grassland and wild flowers to develop, and for those who want a chance to rest for a moment, there is a small picnic area **39**. The character of the walk now begins to change. This section is pleasant and tree shaded, while what had been a very flat landscape to the north becomes ever more undulating. The hill immediately to the left of the walk is so chalky that from a distance it looks almost to be snow covered. The track heads into the woodland, and then narrows down as it goes past a house, to run between more houses. At the edge of the woodland, at a track junction **A** turn right. The path now passes along the edge of the wood with, for a change, grazing land to the side. This area of woodland has been carefully managed, and shows evidence of considerable new planting, rather more birch than the familiar beech. The track steadily steepens, opening up ever wider views, and then enters the wood itself.

Pass a track to the left that leads to Bledlow, then immediately on leaving the wood, look out for a kissing-gate on the right **B**. You will be leaving the wide track and also leaving the line of the Icknield Way, to take the rather indistinct footpath across the field, heading on a diagonal across the face of the hill. After following so many enclosed tracks, it is a real pleasure to walk this footpath across open grassland. The path continues with a line of trees on the left and becomes more obvious. At the corner of the field, go through the kissing-gate and turn right to take the path at the edge of the next field. Cross over the road to the gate opposite and take the obvious path straight across the fields, heading towards the foot of Lodge Hill. This is a very open section of the walk, with an almost complete panoramic view. Cross over a track to a gate, from where the path turns right into the wood **C**. There is a steep little climb through the trees that ends in a grassy

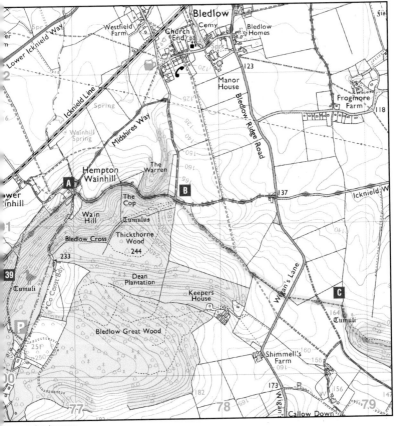

knoll and a magnificent view. On a hilltop up ahead is Lacey Green windmill **40**. This is a smock mill, one in which the sails are mounted on a rotating cap on top of a wooden tower. It is the oldest working example of this type of mill in Britain.

The path now continues as a grassy path, running along the ridge at the top of Lodge Hill. Go through a gate by a group of fine, mature beech, where someone has thoughtfully provided a bench for those who want to take in the view at their leisure, and continue along the crest of the hill. At the end of the ridge, ignore the stile on the right, and take the path on the left going more steeply downhill. The path heads down the valley, with fields to either side, and at the foot of the hill the path swings round to the left, still following the same field boundary down to the road. Cross straight over the road on to the track leading down towards the farm, and take the path immediately to the right of the house garden. After passing large enclosures full of happily pecking hens, you arrive at the edge of a golf course and take the path down to the railway **41**. Cross the line with care, as this is a very busy main line, and although trains whistle to announce their presence it is as well to be aware that they will be travelling at speed. Continue up a little hill to cross over the top of a tunnel, on what appears to be a second railway. They are, in fact, two parts of the same system – the up line and the down line. This was one of the last major routes to be opened in Britain, built to join the Great Central Railway to the GWR. Saunderton tunnel opens out to the impressive 65-foot (20-metre)-deep cutting, built in 1905 and, unlike the earlier cuttings of the 19th century, constructed using steam excavators instead of muscle power.

The path goes straight across the fields to the roadway. Join the road and turn right, rejoining the Icknield Way. At the road junction cross straight over and at the next T-junction **D** cross straight over and turn left along the pavement towards Princes Risborough. Immediately past the sign announcing your arrival at the edge of the town **E**, turn right up a rough track, running between the backs of the houses and the fields. The houses are left behind for a short way. Carry on past the school and cross the new access road for another track along the backs of houses. At the next road junction you can turn left to visit Princes Risborough, otherwise continue straight on along the track opposite. Leaving the houses behind, you come past the sports field and out into the country. Just beyond the playing field **F** turn right onto the footpath, heading up the wooded hill. Over to the left, the chalk has been cut away to create what appears to

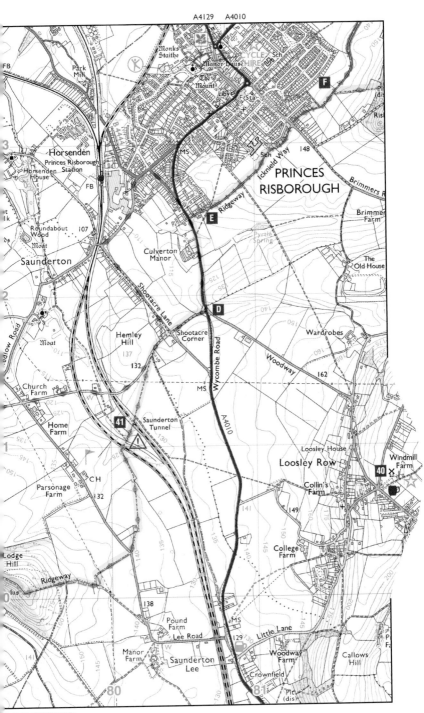

A group of walkers pause to enjoy the view from the hills above Princes Risborough.

be a representation of a dome with a cross on top **42**, known as the Whiteleaf Cross, old but no one seems sure just how old, though it certainly existed as long ago as the 17th century. Once inside the wood, the way up the hill is eased by steps, which climb up to emerge in grassland with a seat to enjoy the view out over the town. An obvious path leads to the road and then does not continue across the stile, but turns left to follow the edge of the next patch of woodland. Look out for a pair of beech trees which have intergrown, winding their trunks together. Reaching the road, continue up it to the right for a short way then turn left **G**.

You are now on a broad track with a large picnic area to the side, still running along the edge of the wood. At the next crossing carry straight on into the Whiteleaf Nature Reserve, shown on the map as heavily wooded but devastated by the 1990 storms, though at the time of writing a restoration programme was well under way. As part of the work, a New Stone Age barrow is being conserved, and for once one can see how these structures must have looked originally – startlingly white chalk mounds. A walk to the escarpment edge provides an opportunity to peer down at the chalk cross. The track now swings away to the right towards more woodland.

This is a particularly fine example of Chiltern summit woodland, with the route following a broad track, while a beautiful wooded valley opens out on the right. Having reached the summit of the hill, the track inevitably starts to descend again towards the valley road. At the road turn left past The Plough at Cadsden – a pub which not only offers refreshment but tells you where you are as well. The owners very helpfully offer a special service to visiting walkers: rather than take off their muddy boots, they can select a pair of carrier bags to put over them and then shuffle inside. Take the first turning into the woods **H** which leads to a steep climb to grassland, almost encircled by woodland. This is a delightful section, with grassland, good views and pleasant paths that are a joy to walk over. The path now goes into scrubby woodland and continues straight on at the next track-crossing to the gate; on coming through the gate take the path on the left **I**. For those not yet sated with Iron Age hill forts, Pulpit Hill fort can be visited by means of a very steep climb up a path on the right. The track continues up some cut steps to an old tree-lined sunken way. Cross this and look out for the kissing-gate on the left.

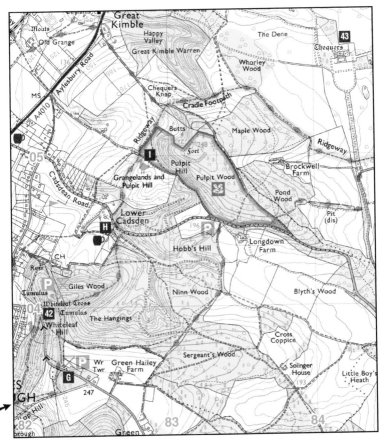

Contours are given in metres
The vertical interval is 5m

The path now begins to go diagonally downhill past a huge, spreading beech tree. Turn right on the grassy path that passes along the head of a valley, then dips down into a ditch, which is presumably associated with the hill fort. The path now levels out above the head of a valley, which drops precipitously away down a beautiful wooded hillside, and the name Happy Valley seems very appropriate. Passing through a gate, carry straight on across the field, and at the next gate the path emerges at the edge of the Chequers estate. The house **43,** originally built in the 16th century**,** was given in 1917 by Lord Lee of Fareham for the use of the Prime Minister as a country home. The walk itself runs along the estate boundary beside the woodland. At the edge of the wood turn left to take a path straight across the parkland, passing over the tree-lined drive near the two gatehouses, to reach the road. Cross straight over and take the track to the left of the houses heading into the next patch of woodland. The route goes down through the line of trees, and there is a convenient footpath next to the rutted track. As the footpath ends, the route continues via a deep sunken path heading up the hill and carries on across a bridleway. At the top of the hill, turn left on to the footpath, just above a ditch. The path follows a somewhat wayward route through the woods, but there are acorn waymarks along the route, and in general it is not difficult to follow.

At the road **J** turn right and leave the B-road at the far end of the woodland, turning left to take the path into the wood. The path winds through the trees, with occasional glimpses through to the valley, and after the path has swung first right and then left the view really does open up to the countryside around Ellesborough. The path now heads to the top of Coombe Hill and the monument to the men of Buckinghamshire who were killed in the Boer War **44**. Sadly, at some time, the original bronze plaque was stolen, and the names are now carved in stone. This is a splendid viewpoint, and a panorama has pointers to all the places that you might see, though for some of them the air would need to be exceptionally clear. From the monument, take the broad green path to the right, cross over a sunken way and take the rather flinty path heading gently downhill. At the woodland, turn left to continue down the hill and where the way divides continue the descent by the path on the left. Turn right at the road, and follow it down into Wendover.

Coombe Hill monument commemorates local men who died in the Boer War.

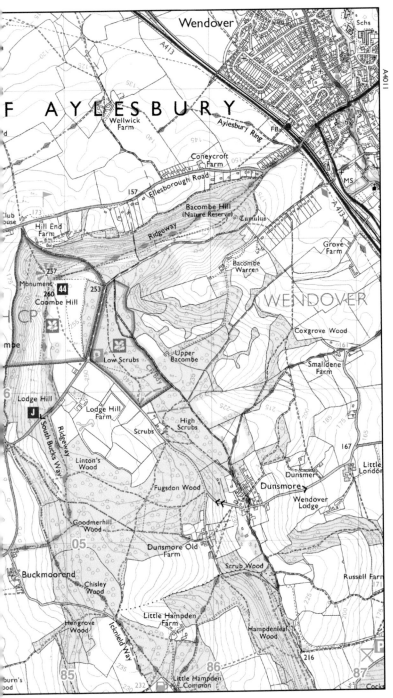

ours are given in metres
vertical interval is 5m

Ancient tracks

Almost every account of the Ridgeway describes it as an ancient track, but the bald statement still leaves several questions unanswered. How old is ancient? Does the Ridgeway National Trail actually follow the same line as some prehistoric route? And, most importantly of all, how do we know it really is ancient?

The first point to note is that we are talking about tracks not roads. In prehistory, the only tracks that can be definitely established and dated are those such as the wooden plank paths through swampy land, as in the Somerset Levels. The Ridgeway has no surface features that can be recognised as the work of early man and so there are no physical remains that can be dated. There is, however, considerable evidence that after the last great ice age, animals migrated over large areas of the country, often in sizeable groups, and would have taken the easiest routes, spreading out in open country and converging at fords and passes. These natural migration routes could well have formed the basis for later human tracks: not narrow pathways, but broad, scarcely defined ways. At one time, it was thought that the presence of so many obvious archaeological sites along the line of routes such as the Ridgeway provided strong evidence of its importance. These range from the barrows of the New Stone Age and Bronze Ages to the hill forts and field systems of the Iron Age. We now know, largely due to aerial photography, that the patterns are not that simple. The ploughs used in the valleys destroyed many sites, while on the uplands, largely given over to grazing, the monuments were left undisturbed. The low outlines of ancient field boundaries are still visible, for example, on the Marlborough Downs; the outlines of similar fields in the nearby valleys can be seen only by close examination of photographs taken from the air. What we do have, however, is the firm evidence that materials were moved around. Clusters of stone axes have been found along both the Icknield Way and the Ridgeway, some of the axes coming from as far away as the Lake District. The argument that a site such as the Windmill Hill camp might be an old trading centre has been strengthened by the discovery of pots made from clays only available from regions as far away as Cornwall. As the New Stone Age gave way to the Bronze Age, trade seems to have increased, not just within Britain but with continental Europe as well.

So, the evidence that early man wandered far and wide is clear, and logic would suggest that the wanderers opted for the easiest route. The chalk ridge was an obvious line to follow, clear of the valleys, which for centuries were densely forested and often waterlogged. The Romans gave us the first documented roads, but these were their own well-constructed highways, and it was left to the Anglo Saxons to offer a classification of all kinds of path and track, among which are some described as being already old. These include a group known as *hyrcgweg*, which can be translated as ridgeways, and our Ridgeway is one of these. So, at the very least, we can say with confidence that it was already ancient in the Dark Ages. Out of a total of over 1,500 roads described in charters, only a few are given names, suggesting that they were of special importance, and among these was Icknield Street in Berkshire. It is safe to assume that if this part of the Icknield Way was important, then its connection, the Ridgeway, would have been no less so. Yet for all the centuries of use, it seems no one defined how wide the way was or exactly where it went until the 18th century. Before that, drovers could allow their animals to roam over wide areas as they made their way along the ridge, while individuals simply followed the rough line of the way. Then the Enclosure Acts parcelled up the old common land between various owners, with a defined space left for the Ridgeway. It varied in width from 12 to 20 metres and was bordered by hedgerows and fences. It was now officially a highway which had to be kept open to all. When the legislation was passed, no one had thought of motorbikes, let alone 4-wheel drives, which would romp along the free highway, taking advantage of these old rights and privileges.

We are fortunate that the Ridgeway still has much of the character of an ancient green lane, and that since 1972 it has been a National Trail which we can walk, just as our forebears have done not just for centuries but for millennia.

6 Wendover to Ivinghoe Beacon

via Tring
11 ¹/₂ miles (18.6 km)

Wendover town centre is approached via a bridge crossing over the main road and the railway, and the route continues straight down the main street. This is an attractive little town, with a good mixture of buildings, including quite a number with timber framing, infilled with brick, a technique known by the rather charming name of 'nogging'. There is a small market square, where happily markets are still held. Where the road swings round to the left by the clock-tower **A,** turn right down the path, signposted to St Mary's Church, passing a multi-gabled building with an unusual chimney, in which two separate flues meet in an inverted U. The path emerges in a small park beside a clear stream. Where the stream tumbles over a little weir, the path turns away past a pond. This strongly suggests the presence of a water mill at some time, and records do show a mill on the site in medieval times. The path now heads off towards the church, a rather grand affair with a square, buttressed flint tower. On reaching the church, turn left down the road past another set of buildings suggestive of old industrial use **45**. Look, for example,

Old thatched houses add charm to a Wendover street.

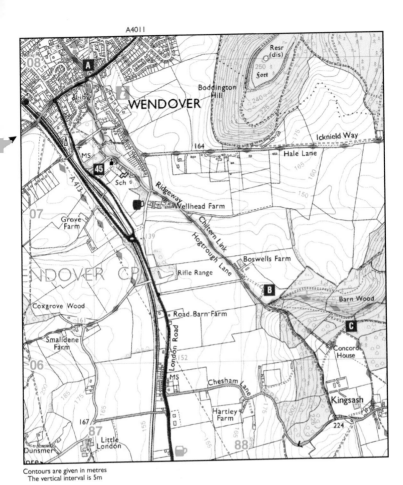

Contours are given in metres
The vertical interval is 5m

how the lower part of one corner has been rounded to allow wagons to negotiate the turn without damaging the brickwork.

At the T-junction, carry straight on to the track opposite, leading up to Wellhead Farm, beyond which the track becomes somewhat rougher and continues straight on to the woodland. At the edge of the wood **B** take the track round to the left to an area which has been planted with conifers. The paths soon divide and you take the path to the right, heading steadily uphill on a long diagonal into an area of broadleaved woodland with birch well represented alongside the familiar beech, all laid out in neat rows. At the top of the rise, where paths divide, take the level path swinging round to the left **C**. This becomes a pleasant, firm path through mixed woodland, with just the occasional glimpse of the open land to the east.

125

The Ridgeway lives up to its name at the eastern end, as it follows a dramatic, high-level route.

On reaching the road, turn right and immediately left through a gate to continue the woodland walk, which now begins to go back downhill. On reaching a second path, turn left to go more steeply downhill along a hollow way. At the bottom of the hill, cross over the track and take the steps down to a deep hollow way **D** and turn right up it. This is a steady climb now, with the view lost behind the steep banks to either side.

The woodland ends at the road. Cross straight over through a kissing-gate for a walk across the fields, with a prominent landmark up ahead in the shape of a telecommunications mast. At the road turn left then immediately right for the next patch of woodland, passing an immense chalk pit on the left. The broad path leads along the edge of the wood to a road, where you turn left, continuing the walk in the same general direction. At the next road junction, carry straight on down Church Lane, passing

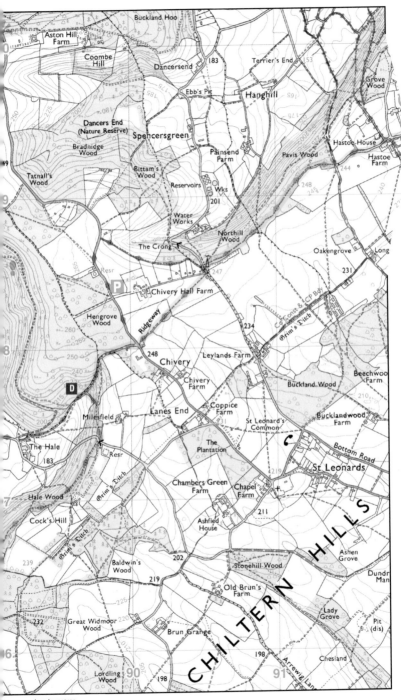

Aston Hill Farm
Coombe Hill
Buckland Hoo
Dancersend 183
Terrier's End 153
Grove Wood
Ebb's Pit
Hanghill
Dancers End (Nature Reserve)
Spencersgreen
Painsend Farm
Pavis Wood
Hastoe House
Hastoe Farm
Bradnidge Wood
Bittam's Wood
244
Tatnall's Wood
Reservoirs
Wks
201
248
249
Water Works
Northill Wood
Oakengrove
Long
The Crong
247
231
Resr
P
Chivery Hall Farm
234
Grim's Ditch
Hengrove Wood
Ridgeway
260
250
248
Chivery
Leylands Farm
Beechwood Farm
D
Chivery Farm
Buckland Wood
210
Milesfield
Lanes End
Coppice Farm
St Leonard's Common
Bucklandwood Farm
The Hale
183
Resr
The Plantation
219
St Leonards
Bottom Road
Grim's Ditch
Chambers Green Farm
Chapel Farm
211
Hale Wood
Cock's Hill
Ashfied House
Ashen Grove
Grim's Ditch
239
Baldwin's Wood
202
Stonehill Wood
Dundr Man
219
Old Brun's Farm
232
Great Widmoor Wood
Brun Grange
Lady Grove
Pit (dis)
Lordling Wood
90
198
CHILTERN
198
91
Arrewig Lan
Chesland

HILLS

tours are given in metres
e vertical interval is 5m

127

a group of estate cottages, dated 1903. Beyond that at Hastoe Cross, turn left and take the track to the right off the road, heading once again into woodland. This is again a broad, stony track heading slightly downhill through Tring Park. This becomes a long, straight track down an avenue of lime trees, planted by the Rothschild family in the late 19th century. Their former mansion can be seen down in the valley and is now the Arts Educational School. Walkers may see what looks like a small grey squirrel, but with large black eyes: not in fact a squirrel at all but a glis-glis, another Rothschild introduction to the area. This section ends at a continuation of the formal drive to a little classical summerhouse **46**. At the beginning of this drive, turn right down to the road, cross straight over and take the path to the left of the houses and past a trig. point. The footpath goes through a number of gates to a road and continues via a right–left dog-leg to another footpath which heads straight off to the busy A41(T). This is crossed by a high footbridge, which is interestingly built

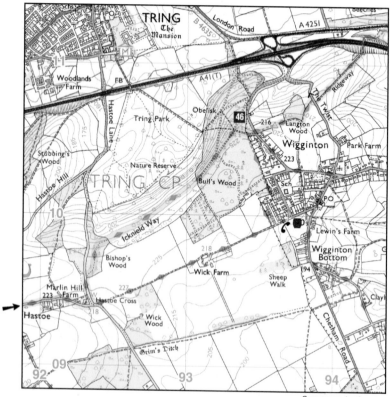

Contours are given in metres
The vertical interval is 5m

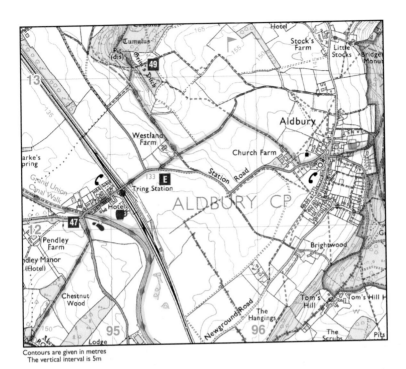

Contours are given in metres
The vertical interval is 5m

with a pronounced slope. At the next road, built on the line of Roman Akeman Street, turn right to cross by the traffic island. Take the narrow footpath, to the right of the house, which leads in a straight line to the road. Turn left, and at the T-junction turn right to take the bridge over the Grand Union Canal **47**, which is the start of a circular walk (page 134). The canal is soon followed by its close neighbour, the railway and Tring station. The line of the canal engineered by William Jessop is closely followed by the line of the railway designed by Robert Stephenson, both choosing to pierce the hills at the same point by deep cuttings. The route of the railway, however, means that Tring station is some considerable distance from the town, hence the need for the large hotel next to it. Carry on along the road, and just past the next road junction **E**, turn left up the metalled farm approach road, then leave the track at the gate to carry straight on along the bridleway. Where tracks cross, turn left on to the tree-lined path which begins to head uphill towards the woodland. Where the tracks fork, take the line to the right into the wood which runs along the top of a somewhat switchbacked ridge. A ditch and bank to the right **49** are part of the Chiltern version of Grim's Ditch, which may well be associated with the earthworks met earlier in the walk. Whether it is or not, it probably served the same function as an Iron Age territorial boundary. The path wanders through the trees, but is well waymarked and easy to follow and eventually emerges in the clear, with views out over Pitstone and its windmill. This is a post mill, the oldest kind of windmill. The sails are attached to the wooden buck, looking rather like a garden shed balanced on a pole. The whole mill has to be turned to bring the sails into the wind.

The path is now gloriously open grassland running along the top of the ridge and for a time following the line of Grim's Ditch, which is now a very distinctive feature. Please note that walkers are asked to stay with the ditch to avoid erosion of the bank. But where the ditch starts to head downhill, leave it and continue straight on at the higher level. The end of the walk is clearly in view at the end of the ridge but, somewhat frustratingly, the path first heads downhill towards the minor road. The official line goes to a point on the road to the right of the car park, then turns left towards it **F**, but it is very tempting to take the path which heads straight to that point. In either case, from the car park, take the obvious path opposite heading uphill once again. The end of the walk is now near and this is a spectacular conclusion. The path heads up the side of the immense, sheer-sided cleft of Incombe Hole, then swings round to the left to pass above it. This is a point to pause and look back over the long line of hills traversed in the course of the walk, as fine a view as any met along the way. Once across the summit, the path again turns to the right and dips down to the road before the last climb of the journey.

Cross over the road and take the track to the right, passing to the right-hand side of the grassy knoll, before joining the very clear path leading up over the grassland to the Beacon **50**. This is the final headland of the Ridgeway and the end of the walk. Archaeology has been something of a feature of the Ridgeway, and it is with us here at the end as well. Although the signs are sparse, there was a hill fort here, and one of the oldest in Britain, begun before the Iron Age, at the end of the Bronze Age. It is a place to linger and enjoy the view, to look at the map on the tablet and congratulate yourself on how far you have come and just to enjoy the pleasures of unspoiled downland, before turning for home. Although the walk is officially over, you still have to get to somewhere else for transport. For those who have arranged to be collected by car, there is a convenient car park beside the minor road, crossed on the way up.

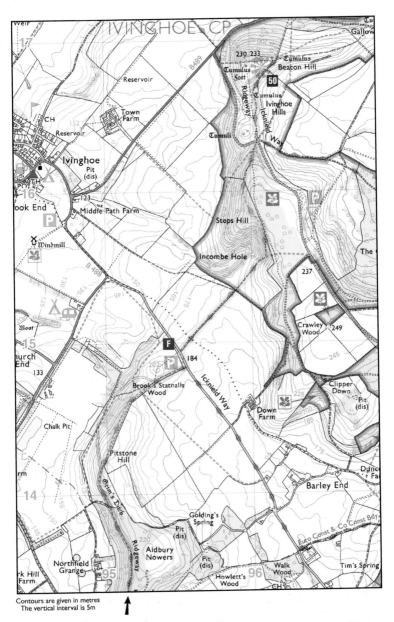

Contours are given in metres
The vertical interval is 5m

A path leads off to the left beside the road to reach it. Those who require public transport should take the path from the trig. point down to the B-road and turn left for Ivinghoe. Most walkers will, I suspect, like the author, be in no hurry to say goodbye to this magnificent National Trail.

The end in sight: the view along the final section of the ridge, leading to Beacon Hill.

A CIRCULAR WALK FROM TRING
5 ¹/₂ miles (9 km)

The walk begins at the bridge over the Grand Union Canal **47**. Take the steps down to the towpath and turn left under the bridge. This is Tring Cutting, a deep slice through the Chilterns, all dug out by hand by an army of navvies. A mile post appears with the letters GJCC, which stand for Grand Junction Canal Company. When work on the canal began in 1793 it was to run from Braunston on the Oxford Canal to Paddington, to complete a through-route between Birmingham and London. It was only incorporated with other canals as the Grand Union in the 20th century. The canal passes a large wharf area with modern factories, followed by a typical Grand Union road bridge. There are memories of the days when all canal traffic was hauled by horses: you can still see the grooves cut by the towropes in the metal bridge guards. Approaching the lock, a number of moored boats can be seen, often including old 70-foot working narrow boats. These come as working pairs: the motor boat, with a rounded stern and metal, swan-neck tiller, pulling the unpowered butty, with pointed stern and wooden rudder. The lock is designed to take two craft, side by side. This is Cow Roast lock, a corruption of 'Cow Rest', a spot where drovers penned their cattle.

At the lock **AA** leave the towpath, passing the brick pump house providing water for the canal, and join the road, turning left and following it as it bends to the right. At the T-junction turn left to cross over the railway, the main line between London and Birmingham. The road continues up towards the big house, Norcott Court, and turns right. At the next junction **BB** turn left to take the road that climbs quite steeply uphill to reach the wood. Carry on into the wood, keeping to the path just inside the edge, which soon turns away to the left, deeper into the wood. At the major track junction **CC** take the track on the left. This is all fine, typical Chiltern woodland and home to a large deer population. Keep on in the same direction and cross straight over the road. Eventually you arrive at a complex of tracks **DD**, and the one to follow is the broad track that runs near the edge of the wood parallel to the valley rim. Continue on this wide track to a path-crossing, then take the narrower path to the right, leading uphill to a clearing. Cross the stile to take the path to the far side of the grassland, then turn left to the Bridgewater monument **48**. The Bridgewater in question is the third Duke, whose 1761 canal from his coal mines at

Worsley into Manchester led to the huge explosion of canal building in the second half of the 18th century. The view is immense and can be improved by climbing the tower, which is open to the public on summer afternoons.

From the monument turn back to the refreshment rooms and take the broad path which swings round to the left. After a short way, turn right on to the sunken track that drops away very steeply down to the village of Aldbury. It emerges in the centre of this idyllic village, with its green and duck pond, with a suitably large duck population. Take the road past the church, and turn right **EE** on to the footpath at the far end of the churchyard. This narrow path runs past the farm and then arrives, still confined, at farmland. At the track junction, turn left and continue on down to the road, rejoining the Ridgeway. The road is now followed past Tring station to the start.

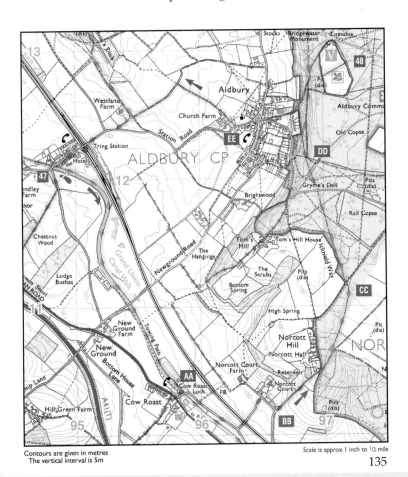

Contours are given in metres
The vertical interval is 5m

Scale is approx 1 inch to ¹/₂ mile

The Tring Cuttings

The Ridgeway provides an interesting opportunity to make a very direct comparison of the solutions chosen by two generations of engineers to the problem of creating a route through the Chilterns. Both had the same overall aim: to provide a modern, efficient transport system to link London and Birmingham.

First on the scene was William Jessop, chief engineer of the Grand Junction Canal, which was later to be incorporated into the Grand Union. Work on the canal began in 1793 and the plans called for locks leading up the eastern slope of the hills through Berkhamsted and more locks plunging down the western side at Marsworth. In between these two watery ladders there had to be a reasonable length of canal to provide water to supply the locks, and this in turn was to be topped up by water from reservoirs at Marsworth. But the land in between the locks rose in a considerable hump, which meant that the canal had to be set in a deep cutting at Tring. You can see this from the road bridge that carries the walk, and when you look down you have to remember that this was created without the help of any mechanical excavators. It was all done by navvies with pick-axe, shovel and barrow.

Just a short way further on the trail brings one to the second bridge, this time over the railway. Work on the London & Birmingham line began in 1833 under the direction of Robert Stephenson. Railway lines do not have to rise through a series of steps like canals, but there is a limit to the gradient that can be climbed – and this was especially true in these pioneering days when the railways were still in their infancy. Stephenson's line stays very close to Jessop's, but disappears briefly into a tunnel at Berkhamsted. At Tring, however, the solution was precisely the same – a deep cutting, but even longer and deeper. It was still dug out by navvies, who had often come straight to the railways from canal work, but we know a good deal more about what was done and how it was achieved. Contemporary accounts reveal that an astonishing 1,400,000 cubic yards of chalk was removed by hand. One famous contractor, Thomas Brassey, calculated that his experienced workers could shift 16 cubic yards a day. Anyone who has ever complained about backache after digging the back garden might contemplate the prospect of digging a trench 3 feet deep, 3 feet across and 15 yards long in a day, and then getting up and doing the same thing again every other day.

Fortunately for posterity, an artist, J. C. Bourne, was on hand to record work on the London & Birmingham Railway. He sketched the workers in the deep cuttings and showed all the technical details of their work. To get the spoil to the surface the men used barrow runs. Planks were laid up the slope to the top of the bank. At the top of each line of planks was a pulley on a post. A rope passed over the pulley, one end of which was fastened to a horse walking along the bank and the other to the barrow. At a signal, the horse walked away and the man walked up the greasy planks balancing the barrow in front of him. At the top of the run, it was tipped into a truck for the spoil to be taken down the line to build the next embankment. The navvy then turned round and galloped back down the run with the barrow at his heels. It was dangerous work and accidents were common. As you look down from these two bridges, the cuttings seem commonplace enough, but just imagine what it must have been like before the vegetation grew back again. These would have been white slashes in the landscape, deep scars that enraged environmentalists of the day, just as motorway construction does their modern successors. John Ruskin was one such campaigner who derided the builders of a railway through Monsal Dale in the Peak District. 'You enterprised a Railroad through the valley – you blasted its rocks away, heaped thousands of tons of shale into its lovely stream . . . and now every fool in Buxton can be at Bakewell in half-an-hour; and every fool in Bakewell at Buxton; which you think a lucrative process of exchange – you Fools Everywhere.'

PART THREE

USEFUL INFORMATION

Transport

Information on transport to and from the Ridgeway can be obtained from Tourist Information Centres. A useful map-based leaflet, showing relevant public transport routes, is available from the Ridgeway National Trail Office (address on page 142) There are also rail and coach centres that will be able to give specific information on timetables.

Rail

National Rail Enquiries: Tel. 08457 484950; www.nationalrail.co.uk

Bus services

National Express: Tel. 08705 808080; www.nationalexpress.com Also or call 0870 6082608, or visit www.traveline.org.uk

Accommodation

A booklet *The Ridgeway National Trail Companion*, giving information on accommodation, is published by the National Trail Office. Information on accommodation can also be obtained from Tourist Information Centres.

Some hostels on or near the route

*Ivinghoe: The Old Brewery House, High Street, Ivinghoe, Beds
    LU7 9EP; Tel. 0870 7705884;
        e-mail ivinghoe@yha.org.uk GR: 165/945161
Streatley on Thames: Hill House, Reading Road, Streatley,
    Berks RG8 9JJ; Tel. 01491 872278;
        e-mail streatley@yha.org.uk GR: 174/591806
*The Ridgeway Centre: Court Hill, Letcombe Regis, Wantage,
    Oxon OX12 9NE; Tel. 01235 760253;
        e-mail info@courthill.org.uk GR 174/393851

* Hostels off route

Tourist Information Centres

Abingdon: Abingdon Information, The Old Abbey House, Abbey Close, Abingdon, Oxon OX14 3JD; Tel. 01235 522711.

Avebury: Avebury Chapel Centre, Green Street, Avebury, Wilts SN8 1RE; Tel. 01672 539179.

Dunstable: Priory House, 33 High Street South, Dunstable, Beds LU6 3RZ; Tel. 01582 590270.

Faringdon: The Pump House, 5 Market Place, Faringdon, Oxon SN7 7HL; Tel. 01367 242191.

Marlborough: The Library, High Street, Marlborough Wiltshire SN8 1HD; Tel. 01672 512663.

Princes Risborough: Tower Court, Horns Lane, Princes Risborough, Bucks HP27 0AJ; Tel. 01844 274795.

Swindon: 37 Regent Street, Swindon, Wilts SN1 1JL; Tel. 01793 530328.

Tring: 99 Akeman Street, Tring, Herts HP23 6AA; Tel. 01442 823347.

Wallingford: Town Hall, Market Place, Wallingford, Oxon OX10 0EG; Tel. 01491 826972.

Wantage: Vale and Downland Museum, 19 Church Street, Wantage, Oxon OX12 8BL; Tel. 01235 760176.

Wendover: Clock Tower, High Street, Wendover, Bucks HP22 6DU; Tel. 01296 696759.

Useful addresses

Berkshire, Buckinghamshire and Oxfordshire Wildlife Trust, The Lodge, 1 Armstrong Road, Littlemore, Oxford OX4 4XT; Tel. 01865 775476; www.bbowt.org.uk

Chiltern Society, The White Hill Centre, White Hill, Chesham HP5 1AG; Tel. 01494 771250; www.chilternsociety.org.uk

English Heritage, www.english-heritage.org.uk
South East: Eastgate Court, 195–205 High Street, Guildford, Surrey GU1 3EH; Tel. 0845 3010 008.
South West: 29 Queen Square, Bristol BS1 4ND Tel. 0845 3010 007.

Friends of The Ridgeway, Chairman Ian Ritchie, The Limes, Oxford Street, Ramsbury, Wilts SN8 2PS; Tel. 01672 520090; e-mail campaign@ridgewayfriends.org.uk www.ridgewayfriends.org.uk

Herts and Middlesex Wildlife Trust, Grebe House, St Michael's Street, St Albans AL3 4SN; Tel. 01727 858901; www.wildlifetrust.org.uk/herts

National Trust, www.nationaltrust.org.uk
  Thames and Solent: Hughenden Manor, High Wycombe, Bucks
  HP14 4LA; Tel. 01494 528051.
  Wessex: Eastleigh Court, Bishopstrow, Warminster, Wilts
  BA12 9HW; Tel. 01985 843600.
Natural England (Headquarters), John Dower House, Crescent
  Place, Cheltenham, Glos GL50 3RA. Tel. 01242 521381.
  Website: www.countryside.gov.uk
Natural England, South East and London Region, Dacre House,
  19 Dacre Street, London SW1H 0DH;
  Tel. 0207 3402900; www.countryside.gov.uk
Ordnance Survey, Romsey Road, Maybush, Southampton
  SO16 4GU, Tel. 08456 050505; www.ordnancesurvey.co.uk
Ramblers Association, 2nd Floor, Camelford House,
  87–90 Albert Embankment, London SE1 7TW;
  Tel. 020 7339 8500; www.ramblers.org.uk
Ridgeway Manager, National Trails Office, Environment and
  Economy, Holton, Oxford OX33 1QQ; Tel. 01865 810224;
  www.nationaltrail.co.uk
Weathercall (Meteorological Office)
  Wiltshire, Glos, Avon: Tel. 09068 5004 05.
  Berks, Bucks and Oxon: Tel. 09068 5004 06.
  Beds, Herts and Essex: Tel. 09068 5004 07.
  www.weathercall.co.uk
Wiltshire Wildlife Trust, Elm Tree Court, Long Street, Devizes,
  Wilts SN10 1NJ; Tel. 01380 725670; www.wiltshirewildlife.org
Youth Hostels Association, Trevelyan House, Dimple Road,
  Matlock, Derbyshire DE4 3YH; Tel. 0870 7708868;
  www.yha.org.uk

Film

A film 'The Ridgeway' presented by Anthony Burton is available
as a download or DVD from www.tvwalks.com

Places to Visit on or near the Ridgeway

Avebury
*Avebury Manor and Garden (NT)
* Stone circles (EH/NT)
*Alexander Keiller Museum and Barn Gallery(EH)
*Silbury Hill (EH/NT)
*West Kennet Avenue and Long Barrow (EH/NT)
*Windmill Hill (NT)

The Sanctuary (EH/NT)
Barbury Castle Country Park
*Ashdown House (NT)
Wayland's Smithy long barrow (NT)
Uffington
* Tom Brown's School Museum, Broad Street
  Uffington Castle (NT)
* White Horse (NT)
*Wantage
  Vale and Downland Museum
*Wallingford
  Wallingford Museum, High Street
  Castle
Streatley
  Basildon Park and Beale Wildlife Park
*Tring
  Walter Rothschild Zoological Museum, Akeman Street
*Ashridge Estate (NT)
  Duke of Bridgewater Monument
*Pitstone
  Windmill (NT)
  Agricultural Museum
*Ivinghoe
  Ford End Watermill

* = off route

Ordnance Survey Maps covering the Ridgeway

Landranger (1:50 000) 165, 173, 174, 175
Explorer (1:25 000) 157, 170, 171, 181